Futures Thinking

Christian Dayé

Futures Thinking

Epistemic Tribes and Territories

Christian Dayé
Graz University of Technology
Graz, Austria

ISBN 978-3-031-91940-4   ISBN 978-3-031-91941-1 (eBook)
https://doi.org/10.1007/978-3-031-91941-1

© The Editor(s) (if applicable) and The Author(s), under exclusive license to Springer Nature Switzerland AG 2025

This work is subject to copyright. All rights are solely and exclusively licensed by the Publisher, whether the whole or part of the material is concerned, specifically the rights of translation, reprinting, reuse of illustrations, recitation, broadcasting, reproduction on microfilms or in any other physical way, and transmission or information storage and retrieval, electronic adaptation, computer software, or by similar or dissimilar methodology now known or hereafter developed.
The use of general descriptive names, registered names, trademarks, service marks, etc. in this publication does not imply, even in the absence of a specific statement, that such names are exempt from the relevant protective laws and regulations and therefore free for general use.
The publisher, the authors and the editors are safe to assume that the advice and information in this book are believed to be true and accurate at the date of publication. Neither the publisher nor the authors or the editors give a warranty, expressed or implied, with respect to the material contained herein or for any errors or omissions that may have been made. The publisher remains neutral with regard to jurisdictional claims in published maps and institutional affiliations.

Cover Pattern © Harvey Loake

This Palgrave Macmillan imprint is published by the registered company Springer Nature Switzerland AG.
The registered company address is: Gewerbestrasse 11, 6330 Cham, Switzerland

If disposing of this product, please recycle the paper.

To Paul and Theodor

Acknowledgments

Roughly a decade ago, Werner Reichmann introduced me to the literature on social scientific foresight and encouraged me to pursue scientific approaches to futures thinking as the topic for my research. I owe him thanks for this. Further, I am indebted to Roman Lukas Prunč, from my research unit at Graz University of Technology, who not only helped me solve technical problems with the data but was also an important sounding board for my ideas on futures thinking over various joint research and teaching activities. Finally, the support of Mitsuhiro Tada from Kumamoto University in providing a correct transcription of the Japanese proverb quoted in Chap. 1 is gratefully acknowledged, as is the support of Marek Skovajsa (Prague), Andreas Unterweger (Leibnitz), and George Gussenhoven (Graz) in checking, for Chap. 7, the translations of Beheim's proverb into Czech, Dutch, and Slovenian.

I also wish to thank Rachael Ballard and Vinoth Kuppan, both from Palgrave Macmillan/Springer, for their patience in accompanying me through the writing of this book.

The book was written while I was working at the STS—Science, Technology and Society Unit of Graz University of Technology, Austria. I am grateful for the support I received from the Unit's members throughout the years. In terms of its contents, the book took shape in the vibrant intellectual environment of the research platform Zukunft–Technik–Gesellschaft (Z-T-G), a collaboration between Graz University of Technology and the University of Graz that I have the honor to head since its foundation in 2023. Last, not least, I gratefully acknowledge several cohorts of students in my courses on futures studies at Graz University of Technology, whose critical questions continuously force me to sharpen my ideas on the nature of the future, sociology, and futures thinking.

While the empirical studies, the data, the theoretical framework, and the research questions presented in this book have not been published before, I have at times drawn on supporting arguments developed in earlier publications, the majority of which appeared in German. Of these, I specifically want to mention:

- Dayé, Christian. 2017. Soziologische Konzeptualisierungen von wissenschaftlichen Kollektiven und ihr Einsatz in der Soziologiegeschichte. In *Handbuch Geschichte der deutschsprachigen Soziologie*, ed. Stephan Moebius and Andrea Ploder, 2:63–80. Springer Reference Sozialwissenschaften. Wiesbaden: Springer VS. https://doi.org/10.1007/978-3-658-07999-4_2-2.
- Dayé, Christian. 2023. Die Erschließung der Zukunft: Unsicherheit als Motor der Sozialwissenschaften. In *Soziologie und Krise: Gesellschaftliche Spannungen als Motor der Geschichte der Soziologie*, ed. Nicole Holzhauser, Stephan Moebius, and Andrea Ploder, 219–234. Wiesbaden: Springer. https://doi.org/10.1007/978-3-658-35204-2_9.
- Dayé, Christian. 2024. A Movement Matured: Results of a Co-citation Analysis, and Some Reflections on the Relations Between Social Structure and Ideas in Futures Studies. *World Futures Review* 16. SAGE Publications Inc: 181–198. https://doi.org/10.1177/19467567231170822.
- Dayé, Christian. 2025. "Zukunft in der Soziologie. Vermessungen einer komplizierten Beziehung." Forthcoming in *Interdisziplinarität und Zukunftsforschung*, ed. Axel Zweck, Karlheinz Steinmüller, Tim Franke, and Katharina Schäfer.

February 2025   Graz

Competing Interests The author has no competing interests to declare that are relevant to the content of this manuscript.

Contents

1 Introduction   1

2 A Short History of Futures Studies, and Its Relations to Sociology   13

3 The Sociology of Scientific Collectives: A Conceptual Overview   35

4 Researching Scientific Attention Spaces: Epistemic Tribes and Territories   57

5 Epistemic Tribes and Territories in Futures Studies   69

6 Epistemic Tribes and Territories in the Sociology of the Future   83

7 Conclusion: The Future of Futures Thinking in the Social Sciences   99

Author Index   117

Subject Index   121

ABOUT THE AUTHOR

Christian Dayé is a sociologist of knowledge, science, and technology at Graz University of Technology in Austria. A prolific author, he received the 2022 Distinguished Scholarly Publication Award of the Section History of Sociology & Social Thought of the American Sociological Association for his monography *Experts, Social Scientists, and Techniques of Prognosis in Cold War America* (2020, Palgrave Macmillan). With Mark Solovey, he co-edited the widely acclaimed volume *Cold War Social Science: Transnational Entanglements* (2021, Palgrave Macmillan).

LIST OF FIGURES

Fig. 5.1	Co-citation network of futures studies	72
Fig. 5.2	Overlay visualization of futures studies' epistemic territories	80
Fig. 6.1	Frequency of terms "future" and "futures" in titles of articles published in sociological journals, 1908–2023 (N = 988)	85
Fig. 6.2	Share (in %) of articles with terms "future" or "futures" in the title among the overall output in sociological journals	86
Fig. 6.3	Co-citation network of the sociology of the future	87
Fig. 6.4	Overlay visualization of epistemic territories in the sociology of the future	96

LIST OF TABLES

Table 2.1	Key assumptions of futures studies according to Bell (2003)	21
Table 3.1	Concepts of scientific collectives according to their analytical foci	36
Table 4.1	Data characteristics	65
Table 5.1	The first co-citation cluster in futures studies	73
Table 5.2	The second co-citation cluster in futures studies	74
Table 5.3	The third co-citation cluster in futures studies	75
Table 5.4	The fourth co-citation cluster in futures studies	75
Table 5.5	The fifth co-citation cluster in futures studies	75
Table 5.6	The co-occurrence clusters of futures studies	78
Table 6.1	The first co-citation cluster in the sociology of the future	88
Table 6.2	The second co-citation cluster in the sociology of the future	89
Table 6.3	The third co-citation cluster in the sociology of the future	90
Table 6.4	The co-occurrence clusters of the sociology of the future	92

CHAPTER 1

Introduction

Abstract This introductory chapter starts from the insight that within the social sciences, two knowledge collectives are concerned with the study of the future. The two collectives are futures studies and the sociology of the future. While basically all science produces some form of knowledge about the future, it is these two that explicitly concern themselves with describing and analyzing futures beyond the sphere of the individual or the single system, but with futures of the world or of humanity. From this insight, this chapter proceeds to introduce the objective of the book: to explain this bipartite institutionalization with reference to historical processes in the social sciences; building on this exploration of their roots, to explore by empirical means how the attention spaces of the two knowledge collectives are structured; and to derive, in concluding, how futures thinking in the social sciences might, and should, be organized in the near future.

Keywords Futures studies • Sociology of the future • Foresight • Future • Utopia

INTRODUCTION

This book is about fields in the social sciences that explicitly concentrate on studying the future. It starts from the somewhat puzzling finding that there is not just one, but at least two such fields: futures studies and the

© The Author(s), under exclusive license to Springer Nature Switzerland AG 2025
C. Dayé, *Futures Thinking*,
https://doi.org/10.1007/978-3-031-91941-1_1

sociology of the future.[1] After a brief and cursory exploration of the historical developments behind this bipartite institutionalization, the large part of the book focuses on describing the two knowledge collectives as epistemic tribes and territories. These concepts are introduced as the available conceptualizations do not convincingly capture the actual social forms and dynamics at play in the two knowledge collectives. Also, they allow for a better alignment with the empirical data used. Based on scientometric analyses, the book compares the key references and sources that members of the knowledge collectives use in crafting and developing their arguments—resulting in different clusters, that is, *epistemic tribes*—as well as the topics discussed within these fields—that is, the *epistemic territories* they claim.

Why is this relevant? We live in times where the future of humanity is at stake. "The future's uncertain and the end is always near," as Jim Morrison put it. Grabbing a beer might help some of us coping with the uncertainty, at least temporarily, but it will not make go away the fact that the extinction of all living things on earth is not just a possible, but indeed a probable future (Tonn 2021). As futurist Jennifer Gidley (2017, 1) dryly notes, "The future we face today is one that threatens our very existence as a species." In searching for ways to avoid falling into the abyss, it is wise to make use of the potentials of the sciences—not in terms of expecting science to deliver more technology to solve problems that technological progress created in the first place; not in terms of telling us how the future will look like; but rather by using their methodological arsenals of sober research and analysis as well as their institutionalized spaces of critical reflection to create images of possible futures that are socially and environmentally sustainable. Since avoiding the imminent extinction requires collective action, shared images of the future can have existential orientational impact—provided that they are fact-based.

As fields engaging in research on images of the future, futures studies and the sociology of the future thus can play a vital role in our ongoing efforts to find ways toward a better future for humanity (cf. Guéguen and Jeanpierre 2022). At the same time, understanding their social shape and intellectual reference points is important to better interpret their

---

[1] In recent years, the future has also received some attention within anthropology (Bryant and Knight 2019). Yet, as these are only recent developments, the focus on comparing futures studies and the sociology of the future, both fields of scientific publication with longer track records, appears justified.

approaches and evaluate their potentials. The book thus presents studies in the sociology of knowledge of two scientific fields primarily concerned with the future; yet, its objective is not to "objectify the objectifying subject," as Pierre Bourdieu (1988, xii) understood it, but rather to explore the intellectual traditions in which these two fields move and the social forms within which they carry out their research in order to better understand each of the fields' contributions—and perhaps the differences between them.

But isn't any science inherently trying to say something about the future? Isn't the main function of a scientific law to provide us with the ability to predict? If so, what allows us then to single out futures studies and the sociology of the future? These questions are addressed in the following sections, before the chapter concludes with an overview of the argument developed in the book.

Foresight and the Idea of the Future

Foresight is an essential ingredient of human action. As the term is used in sociology (and other social sciences), an action is an intentional behavior aimed at a certain purpose. In the words of Max Weber (1978, 4), "We shall speak of 'action' insofar as the acting individual attaches a subjective meaning to his behavior—be it overt or covert, omission or acquiescence." Action is thus always based on a reasoned decision. A decision, first, implies that other courses of action are possible, at least in principle. In order to decide between various courses of action, one has to develop some ideas about their possible consequences. Behavioral psychologists have explored this type of thinking as *foresight* (Bulley et al. 2017; Suddendorf et al. 2022). Obviously, such an individual form of foresight is not a characteristic of modern society. Rather, it must be understood as a precondition of human culture, thus being a part of human life on this planet for thousands of years.[2]

Presumably as old, however, is the doubt about the veracity of human foresight. The reasons behind this doubt have been manifold and subject to historical and cultural change. Isn't it preposterous to think that the Gods let the mortals see their plans? Why should Nature stick with the

---

[2] Whether or not non-human animals are able to engage in those forms of mental time travel required for foresight is still not fully clear (Suddendorf and Corballis 2007, 2010; Inkeller et al. 2024).

conformities that the human-made laws install on it? How to account for all the things and happenings beyond our knowledge and control? *Rainen no koto o ieba Oni ga warau*, a Japanese proverb goes: Talk about tomorrow and the Oni, demons in Japanese folklore, will laugh.[3] The need for foresight in making good decisions is in a constant tension with the doubts that accompany it—doubts that come from experience of things that did not work out as planned. It is thus not surprising that societies and cultures have provided various means to cope with this uncertainty—ranging from myths to religion, from superstition to science.

The uncertainty related to foresight only increases if one moves the perspective from the individual to the future of a social collective more generally. The differentiation between individual foresight or prognoses and a more comprehensive notion of *the* future is crucial for understanding the particularities of futures studies and the sociology of the future. When we talk with others about "the future," we usually do not talk about their individual plans. To put it bluntly, *their* possible future (or yours, or mine) is not the same thing as *the* future. And while it is true that one of the hopes that societies across the centuries invested in science (and other forms of prediction) was that it could produce valid prognoses, it is also true that for the most part, such prognoses concerned only specific phenomena (and *their* futures), not *the* future.

The idea that science should also concern itself with studying *the* future only emerged in the early twentieth century, when the hopes that had been invested in science as a means to decrease uncertainty met with the newly awakened perception of the disastrous impact of technological progress on the environment, and hence society. Of course, that doesn't mean that the future had not been an object of scholarly interest already before. To the contrary, throughout the centuries, historians and philosophers had indeed speculated about the world of the future, a scholarly endeavor that eventually has been called macrohistory or big history (cf. Galtung and Inayatullah 1997; Christian 2022). But the notion that what was needed was a new science particularly dedicated to studying the future—or various futures—had not been put forth.

While the birth and early development of futures studies, and its relations to the sociology of the future, are discussed in Chap. 2, the next section focuses on a precondition for the claim for a science of the future.

---

[3] I thank Mitsuhiro Tada, professor of sociology at Kumamoto University, for helping me with the transcription into Latin alphabet.

This precondition is that there exists an idea of the future. While foresight might be a necessary element of any human action, the idea of the future is not an anthropological constant, but emerged in a century-long process of cultural development. Only after the idea of the future, and a notion of science, had been culturally anchored, could the claim for a science of the future be put forth.

The Future: An Idea and Its History

A major evidence for the fact that unlike individual foresight, the idea of the future has been a relatively recent phenomenon is the fact that throughout ancient history, including the classical antiquity, social rituals of prediction only concerned the possible consequences of individual actions—individual futures. As mentioned above, action is always oriented toward a purpose that may or may not realize as a result of the action. Individual action thus implies a temporal dimension that extends to the future. This temporal dimension of individual action has been the focus of ancient forms of prediction that came mainly in the form of divination (cf. Minois 1998). In a divination, a person who is able to communicate with Gods or spirits conveys their messages to whoever is willing to listen. The clients then try to draw conclusions about whether or not the way of action that they are pondering meets the wishes and the goodwill of the Gods. At the oracle of Delphi in Ancient Greece, for instance, the Gods spoke through the priestess Pythia. Usually, the messages they sent were obscure, a challenge for the listeners who had to decode their meaning. Instead of straightforward sentences about right and wrong, their messages came in riddles.

Similarly, the augurs in Ancient Rome were priests who divined whether or not a proposed course of action found the *placet*, the liking of the Gods, from observing events in nature, for example, the flight of birds. Further, forms of hieroscopy, that is, the divination by inspecting the entrails of sacrificed animals, have been very widespread especially in non-writing cultures.

On all these instances, the question posed to the Gods was not about how *the future* will look like, but about whether or not some course of action was likely to be successful. This was quite in line with a culture that unlike ours had no linear notion of time, but a circular one. Through large parts of the Ancient era up to the Middle Ages, people did not conceive of time as being a steady flow that transforms the present into the past and the future into the present. Rather, in their worlds and in their worldview, things repeated themselves: they went and came back, just like the seasons did (Elias 1997; Gurjewitsch 1997; Huizinga 2006). In cultures where such a circular understanding of time predominated, the future itself was not an issue. True, it was an issue whether or not rain will fall on the fields in the following days. It was an issue whether or not the sea was calm enough to allow for putting the boats to see and go fishing. And perhaps it was an issue whether or not the Gods decided to be merciful those who made them sacrifices. But none of this was decided by the humans. Tomorrow was in the hands of the Gods, and not a result of men's decisions and actions. After winter came spring and summer and fall, and winter again, as long as it pleased the Gods.

These, then, are three important characteristics of our modern idea of the future: (1) the world is changing, and it will be different in the future from what we have experienced in the past; and (2) parts of these changes the future is, in parts at least, a result of what we human beings do today and have done before. This idea is not so old and widespread as it may seem from today's viewpoint; with an—admittedly restricted—view on the history of European thought, it emerged only in the late seventeenth century (Hölscher 2016). The notion that the future of mankind on Earth was not in the hands of the Gods alone, but that it followed from what people do, and, more precisely, that it followed directly from their actions and not from the reactions of the Gods—this notion has been an important step toward the concept of the future that we have today.

Roughly around the same time when this notion of consequences emerged in European history, a specific new literary genre made its appearance, a genre that is nowadays known as utopia. This term was taken from the title of the first book in this genre, written by English writer and lawyer Sir Thomas More (1478–1535) or, in his Latin name, Thomas Morus, who in 1516 published *A little, true book, not less beneficial than enjoyable, about how things should be in the new island Utopia*. The book described an imaginary society that is rationally organized. On the island Utopia, people did not know private property, hospitals were for free, and divorce was permitted. People lived in cities of no more than six thousand households, each of them having two slaves. Also, the people of Utopia were not waging wars.

Morus's book was the first in a series of well-known books, which all described imaginary societies. The Italian Dominican friar, Tommaso Campanella (1568–1639), wrote about *The City of the Sun*, and the

Englishman Lord Francis Bacon (1561–1626) described his purported travels to *New-Atlantis*. Despite differences, these books share one basic feature so distinct of utopia, namely, that their descriptions of distant societies are meant to function as a mirror and implicit critique of the society in which they had been written. The message of these early utopian books was that a better organization of social and political life was possible. Implicitly, they thus urged people to think about how to change things in order to improve life in their own world.

With regard to the notion of future, it is important to see that in these works, the distance of the utopian society to those of the author is geographical, not temporal. The Ancient Greek term *oútópos*, directly translated as the non-place or the irreal place, was at first a vantage point in space, its distance being measured in miles, not years. This, it should be emphasized, is another indicator of the historical fact that the idea of future as we know it now was not yet developed, a finding that concurs with research that finds that the idea of the present only emerged in the seventeenth century (Landwehr 2014). The idea of the future as a "horizon of expectations" (*Erwartungshorizont*) presupposes the presence of the present as a "space of experience" (*Erfahrungsraum*) (Koselleck 1988a).

The "temporalization of utopia" only took place in the eighteenth century, and it did so along at least two lines. With regard to political and social developments, writers began to imagine a future, more just society (Koselleck 1988b, 2004). This happened to a considerable extent in political theory, and related calls to collective action. The most prominent example of this line of thinking about the future is of course Karl Marx (1818–1883), but under the impression of the disintegration of the *ancien régime* and the overcome social structures on which it had been based, the nineteenth century saw countless authors write theoretical treatises on the society of the future. Utopia now had found a second home in the programs of the then emerging political movements and parties. It did not involve a travel in space anymore, but political action on the spot.

In parallel, a better society continued to be a *topos* in literary writing, yet also here, utopia transformed from a distant place to a distant future. Instead of travelling in space, protagonists began travelling in time. A prominent example for this genre is Edward Bellamy's (1850–1898) novel *Looking Backward: 2000–1887*. The young protagonist of the novel wakes up from a century-long sleep and finds himself in the year 2000, in a society that has nationalized industrial production on a large scale, which allowed for a tremendous reduction of working hours and the possibility to retire at the age of forty-five. This mirrored to some extent the coeval fascination with the power of technology, another characteristic of 19th century utopian writing. Writers began to dream about the progress of science and technology and spell out the impact of this progress on society. On can think, for instance, of Jules Verne's (1828–1905) famous books, who bear proof of the fascination with technological progress when we follow Captain Nemo in his submarine in *Twenty Thousand Leagues Under the Seas* from 1870, or have a canon shoot explorers into outer space in *From the Earth to the Moon* from 1865. These hopeful accounts of the social impact of science and technology of course contrast with other, critical accounts of their potentials, including Mary Shelley's (1797–1851) *Frankenstein* from 1818 or H.G. Wells's (1866–1946) *The Time Machine* from 1895 (see Wagar 1989). We should also note the emergence of the sub-genre of dystopias, where the future brings about danger, the decline of civilizations, and, ultimately, their obliteration—with Robert Hugh Benson's (1871–1914) *Lord of the World* from 1907 or Aldous Huxley's (1894–1963) *Brave New World* as widely received examples.

The nineteenth century also saw the rise of several enterprises specializing in producing forecasts. This, in retrospect, relied on a very fundamental change in perceiving the potential of science, one that was in line with the advances that also inspired the science fiction genre. These new enterprises now applied prognostic techniques from the natural sciences to various phenomena, most importantly to the weather (Harper 2012; Pietruska 2018) and parts of the economy. A very early form of economic forecasts concerned the cotton industry, an industry where in order to organize international trade, it was valuable to have estimates about where how much cotton would be produced over the coming months (Pietruska 2018, ch. 1). Quickly, this industry-specific data was bundled to produce forecasts of the whole economy (Friedman 2014). As regards the weather, the US Army was among the first organizations to entertain a network of trained observers who via telegraph delivered data that was then collected, compared, and used to calculate the "Daily Probabilities" (Pietruska 2018, ch. 2). But clearly, none of these more scientific approaches to prediction tried to describe life in the future in general. Rather, their objective was a short- or mid-term prediction of a specific aspect of life, and in order to render their predictions more stable and trustworthy, they applied scientific techniques, mainly techniques of statistical extrapolation.

All these intellectual works, the scientific prognoses as well as the literary utopias and the images of a future that manifested itself in the countless political treatises published in Europe throughout the eighteenth and nineteenth centuries, shared the same idea of the future, the one we still hold today. In the words of Ossip K. Flechtheim (1971, 16), a pioneer of futures studies introduced in more detail in Chap. 2, this idea is characterized by the following axioms:

1. The world is dynamic, it changes in its basic structures, and it produces new things.
2. Certain basic structures of this change are at least partly cognizable.
3. Direction and speed of this change can in some instances be foreseen in outline.
4. Antithetic prognoses and projections also have their value—they can contribute to the specification of problems and crises and can also be partly correct.
5. Within this frame, there is freedom of choice and there are opportunities for design.
6. The cognition of what is necessary, possible, and wanted co-creates the future.

The developments just described—that is, the appearance of utopias, their temporalization, their entering into the political discourse, and the methodological advances in prognosis among the sciences—built the foundations from which calls for a scientific discipline studying the future emerged. These calls received further energy by pointing to the negative, and partly disastrous, consequences of humanity's technological progress. The massive growth of cities and the destruction of the environment engendered by large-scale industrial mining and production endeavors met with the view of the environment as a complex system of interdependencies pioneered by Alexander von Humboldt (Wulf 2016). Thus, at the core of this call for a scientific study of the future was also the insight that through laying the foundation for technological progress, science was responsible for enabling the large-scale exploitation of our planet. Acknowledging this, the task of science was not only to mitigate desastrous consequences, but also to devise ways into a less exploitative future.

Clearly, future is understood here as a speculative image about the world at large, not about one's own life. It is this character that made the social sciences an obvious place for this new scientific field. The call for a new science thus met with the dynamics of a field that still struggled to stabilize its own academic institutionalization. These dynamics led to a bipartite academic institutionalization of futures thinking in the social sciences: on the one hand, there is the field which is now usually called futures studies—after carrying names such as futurology and futures research (Sardar 2010)—; on the other hand, there has been a small, but steady stream of publications on the future within sociology, the sociology of the future.

The Structure of This Book

The objective of this book is to explore the roots and consequences of the bipartite institutionalization of futures thinking in twentieth-century academia, and beyond. As basically all science produces some future-oriented results, it is paramount to understand that the term futures thinking is used in this book as a complementary term to individual foresight or scientific forecasting of the future of particular, definable system, like next year's cotton production in the United States, or the trajectory of the asteroid Apophis 9942 that is coming close to our planet Earth.

Building on the historical remarks made above, Chap. 2 describes the beginnings of futures studies in more detail and explores how its institutionalization as an international field reverberated with sociology, and vice versa. Chapter 3 proceeds to describe different conceptualizations of knowledge collectives extant in the sociology of science and adjacent fields. This lays the foundation for the theoretical framework and the research design used in the studies on which this book draws; this is done in Chap. 4. Chapter 5 then explores the epistemic tribes and territories of futures studies, while Chap. 6 does the same for the sociology of the future. To anticipate the most important finding: by and large, the two knowledge collectives have hardly any point of overlap. They do not refer to the same sources to corroborate their arguments, and by and large, they are concerned with different future questions. The concluding Chap. 7 speculates about the implications of this apparent division of labor and proposes a possible strategy on how to move forward.

Wherever I cite from a non-English reference, the translation is mine.

References

Bourdieu, Pierre. 1988. *Homo Academicus*. Stanford, CA: Stanford University Press.
Bryant, Rebecca, and Daniel M. Knight. 2019. *The Anthropology of the Future*. New Departures in Anthropology. Cambridge: Cambridge University Press. https://doi.org/10.1017/9781108378277.

Bulley, Adam, Gillian Pepper, and Thomas Suddendorf. 2017. Using Foresight to Prioritise the Present. *Behavioral and Brain Sciences* 40:e79. https://doi.org/10.1017/S0140525X16000996.
Christian, David. 2022. *Future Stories: What's Next?* New York, Boston, London: Little, Brown Spark.
Elias, Norbert. 1997. *Über die Zeit. Arbeiten zur Wissenssoziologie II*, ed. Michael Schröter. Translated by Holger Fliessbach and Michael Schröter. 6. Auflage. stw 756. Frankfurt am Main: Suhrkamp.
Flechtheim, Ossip K. 1971. *Futurologie. Der Kampf um die Zukunft.* 2. Auflage. Köln: Verlag Wissenschaft und Politik.
Friedman, Walter A. 2014. *Fortune Tellers: The Story of America's First Economic Forecasters*. Princeton, Oxford: Princeton University Press.
Galtung, Johan, and Sohail Inayatullah, eds. 1997. *Macrohistory and Macrohistorians: Perspectives on Individual, Social, and Civilizational Change*. Praeger Publishers.
Gidley, Jennifer M. 2017. *The Future: A Very Short Introduction*. Oxford: Oxford University Press.
Guéguen, Haud, and Laurent Jeanpierre. 2022. *La perspective du possible: Comment penser ce qui peut nous arriver, et ce que nous pouvons faire*. Paris: Éditions La Découverte.
Gurjewitsch, Aaron J. 1997. *Das Weltbild des mittelalterlichen Menschen*. 5. Auflage. München: C. H. Beck.
Harper, Kristine C. 2012. *Weather by the Numbers: The Genesis of Modern Meteorology*. Cambridge (MA), London: MIT Press.
Hölscher, Lucien. 2016. *Die Entdeckung der Zukunft*. 2. Auflage. Göttingen: Wallstein.
Huizinga, Johan. 2006. *Herbst des Mittelalters: Studien über Lebens- und Geistesformen des 14. und 15. Jahrhunderts in Frankreich und in den Niederlanden*. 12. Auflage. Stuttgart: Kroener.
Inkeller, Judit, Balázs Knakker, Péter Kovács, Balázs Lendvai, and István Hernádi. 2024. Intrinsic Anticipatory Motives in Non-human Primate Food Consumption Behavior. *iScience* 27:109459. https://doi.org/10.1016/j.isci.2024.109459.
Koselleck, Reinhart. 1988a. "Erfahrungsraum" und "Erwartungshorizont" - zwei historische Kategorien. In *Zur Semantik geschichtlicher Zeiten*, ed. Vergangene Zukunft, 349–375. Frankfurt am Main: Suhrkamp.
Koselleck, Reinhart. 1988b. *Vergangene Zukunft. Zur Semantik geschichtlicher Zeiten*. Frankfurt am Main: Suhrkamp.
Koselleck, Reinhart. 2004. *Futures Past. On the Semantics of Historical Time*. Translated and with an Introduction by Keith Tribe. New York: Columbia University Press.

Landwehr, Achim. 2014. *Geburt der Gegenwart. Eine Geschichte der Zeit im 17. Jahrhundert.* Frankfurt am Main: Fischer.

Minois, Georges. 1998. *Geschichte der Zukunft. Orakel, Prophezeiungen, Utopien, Prognosen.* Translated by Eva Moldenhauer. Düsseldorf, Zürich: Artemis & Winkler.

Pietruska, Jamie L. 2018. *Looking Forward: Prediction & Uncertainty in Modern America.* Chicago: University of Chicago Press.

Sardar, Ziauddin. 2010. The Namesake: Futures; Futures Studies; Futurology; Futuristic; Foresight—What's in a Name? *Futures* 42:177–184. https://doi.org/10.1016/j.futures.2009.11.001.

Suddendorf, Thomas, and Michael C. Corballis. 2007. The Evolution of Foresight: What Is Mental Time Travel, and Is It Unique to Humans? *Behavioral and Brain Sciences* 30:299–313. https://doi.org/10.1017/S0140525X07001975.

Suddendorf, Thomas, and Michael C. Corballis. 2010. Behavioural Evidence for Mental Time Travel in Nonhuman Animals. *Behavioural Brain Research* 215:292–298. https://doi.org/10.1016/j.bbr.2009.11.044.

Suddendorf, Thomas, Jonathan Redshaw, and Adam Bulley. 2022. *The Invention of Tomorrow: A Natural History of Foresight.* New York: Basic Books.

Tonn, Bruce Edward. 2021. *Anticipation, Sustainability, Futures and Human Extinction: Ensuring Humanity's Journey into the Distant Future.* Routledge Research in Anticipation and Futures. London, New York: Routledge, Taylor & Francis Group.

Wagar, W. Warren. 1989. *A Short History of the Future.* University of Chicago Press.

Weber, Max. 1978. Economy and Society: An Outline of Interpretive Sociology. In *Berkeley*, ed. Guenther Roth and Claus Wittich. Los Angeles, London: University of California Press.

Wulf, Andrea. 2016. *The Invention of Nature: Alexander von Humboldt's New World.* New York: Random House.

CHAPTER 2

A Short History of Futures Studies, and Its Relations to Sociology

Abstract Predictions can be found across all fields of science, but in the twentieth century, a separate field became established that concerned itself specifically with describing possible futures: futurology, or future(s) studies. Highlighting several historical episodes, this chapter follows the development of futures studies from the early beginnings in the writings of Ossip K. Flechtheim in the late 1940s to the various attempts to establish the field in the United States, Europe, and Russia in the first half of the twentieth century. It points out that the field only came to fruition as it organized itself as an international endeavor, something that happened after the end of World War II and which drew inspiration from the global impact the detonation of the first nuclear bombs over Japan had. The chapter then proceeds to a discussion of a series of classical contributions from this era. The overarching interest of this reconstruction is to explore the historical roots of the bipartite institutionalization of futures thinking in the social sciences and to identify relations between futures studies and the sociology of the future.

Keywords Futurology • Futuribles • RAND Corporation • Ossip K. Flechtheim • Bertrand de Jouvenel

© The Author(s), under exclusive license to Springer Nature Switzerland AG 2025
C. Dayé, *Futures Thinking*,
https://doi.org/10.1007/978-3-031-91941-1_2

Introduction

Forecasts are made within virtually all sciences, but the vision of having a science responsible for creating comprehensive visions of future human life emerged only in the twentieth century. For reasons that are not completely clear, but may have to do with the relatively minor level of disciplinary institutionalization of sociology in most European countries as well as the wish of the proponents to have this new science integrate knowledge from across all scientific branches, the option of making sociology responsible for providing such comprehensive images of the future never was seriously debated. Not surprisingly, a consequence of this was that the new field struggled had problems to gain recognition from the established academic disciplines. One type of reproach it repeatedly encountered was rooted in coeval philosophy of science. Futures studies (or futurology or futures research) was seen to be at odds with three tenets encapsulating the widely held understanding of what a science is: (*i*) the tenet that empirical observation is a condition sine qua non of every scientific insight; (*ii*) the tenet that science has to observe its objects without interfering with them; and (*iii*) the tenet that science has to stay neutral toward moral judgment and distant to political power.

To begin with (*i*), the impossibility to "know" the future translates into the methodological problem of verification versus confirmation. This is true for all form of predictive statements, or forecasts, in the sciences (for a sociological analysis of this situation, see Reichmann 2018, 251–287). While scientific statements about the present and the past can be verified by systematic empirical observation and measurement, this is not possible with predictive statements. Instead, it has been argued, the procedure with predictive hypotheses is not verification, but confirmation (Hempel and Oppenheim 1945; Helmer and Rescher 1959). However, when the objective is to go beyond forecasts of well-defined singular processes and to develop a comprehensive vision of future human life, confirmation also is illusionary, due to the impenetrable complexity of the involved processes. Thus, futures studies perforce involve a considerable amount of (expert) opinion and speculation. This opens avenues for criticisms.

The second tenet (*ii*) that futures studies appear to violate concerns its interference with its objects. However, this also applies to many predictions in the social realm. Convincing statements about the future have the potency to shape our decisions, and predictions can therefore have a causal effect insofar as they increase the likelihood of having realized those events or developments that they themselves predicted. In sociology, this phenomenon is known as the mechanism of self-fulfilling prophecies (and its counterpart, self-destroying prophecies): a prediction becomes true just *because* it has been publicly proclaimed (Merton 1948). It is therefore true that if a prediction is verified in hindsight, this has to some degree been a mere consequence of its having been publicly proclaimed.

A third tenet (*iii*) that fueled the concerns of those who opposed futures studies' establishment as a science follows from the openness of the future, more precisely, from the responsibility that comes with this openness. Futures studies, it has been argued, can never be completely neutral toward its object, since it is not only about knowing the future, it is also about shaping it. If, as argued in Chap. 1, one central aspect of our modern idea of the future is that it is shaped by what people did in the recent past and do today, then we have the possibility—and perhaps, the duty—to think about how we want to live and about how we design the process to arrive there. These, to be sure, are fundamentally questions of morality. And the means of science, the critics emphasized, are inappropriate to solve moral problems—they can support the search for solutions, but not make the decision.[1]

Struggles over its scientific character accompanied the history of the field from its very beginning, and it is safe to say that none of those who in the middle of the twentieth century contributed to its theoretical formation approached this endeavor naively. In other words, while they were convinced about the timeliness of the science they promoted, and at times enthusiastically about its potentials, they were also aware of the intricacies implied in their project.

The Intellectual Birth and Baptism of a New Science: Ossip K. Flechtheim, Robert Jungk, Dennis Gabor

While musings about the need for a new science of the future can already be found in writings from the nineteenth century, the first more systematic attempt toward academic establishment is closely linked to Ossip

---

[1] An interesting take on this situation has been the literature on trans-science, that is, on questions that come in the form of a scientific problem but ultimately address moral convictions (e.g., Weinberg 1972; Eyal 2019).

K. Flechtheim (1909–1998).[2] Flechtheim was born in Mykolaiv (Миколаїв, Ukraine), but his family moved back to their former hometown Münster (Germany) in 1910 and, a few years later, to Düsseldorf. He studied law and administrative science (*Rechts- und Staatswissenschaften*) in Freiburg im Breisgau, Heidelberg, Paris, and Berlin, and successfully defended a dissertation on Hegel's theory of punitive law at the University of Cologne in 1934 (Keßler 2007). Soon after, he left Germany for Switzerland before emigrating, with support of the also exiled Institut für Sozialforschung directed by Max Horkheimer, to New York City.

In the United States, he held various short-term university appointments, but a permanent position never materialized, mainly because he had been in touch with the communist party in Germany and still held leftist views. Through the agency of political scientist Franz Neumann, whom Flechtheim had supported during the writing of his influential study on Nazism, *Behemoth* (Neumann 1942), Flechtheim was appointed professor at the *Deutsche Hochschule für Politik* in 1952, an organization for political science that became part of the Freie Universität Berlin in 1959. He stayed at FU Berlin, eventually becoming emeritus professor in 1974.

Among other contributions to the scientific study of the future, Flechtheim gave the new science a name: futurology. He had first proposed this name in a letter to a friend in 1942 (cf. Keßler 2011, 245), and then mentioned it *en passant* in a footnote to an article on the theories of history of Arnold J. Toynbee, Max Weber, and Alfred Weber (Flechtheim 1943). A full definition of the term appeared in an 1945 article under the title "Teaching the Future" (Flechtheim 1966a). In Flechtheim's understanding, futurology was a very broad endeavor that aimed to go beyond more specific and restricted predictions from the various sciences. By synthesizing them, and by adding speculative imagination, futurology set out to explore "the destiny of man, the future of his society, and the tomorrow of his culture" (Flechtheim 1966b, 71). Futurology had to be more than utopia, technocracy, or crisis management; rather, it had to integrate scientific prognosis, social planning, and a deep engagement with philosophical and ethical questions (Flechtheim 1969, 264; cf. Flechtheim 1971, 9).

---

[2] A valuable source for earlier writings is the introductory sections of Flechtheim's book *Futurologie. Möglichkeiten und Grenzen* [*Futurology: Potentials and Limits*] (Flechtheim 1968, 7–18).

To Flechtheim, the creation of this new science was a historical necessity. The crisis of humanity that came with the entry of the world into the nuclear age, and specifically with the detonation of the atomic bombs over Hiroshima and Nagasaki in 1945, provided a fertile soil for it. Given the obvious urgency of the demand for knowledge about the future, Flechtheim was not overly concerned about whether futurology qualified as a science. He admitted that if exactness were a criterion of science, then futurology better be treated as a "'prescientific' branch of knowledge" (Flechtheim 1966b, 76). But perhaps, this was not a correct definition of science, and an alternative, more comprehensive definition had to be found.[3]

While the crises that humanity had to face in the middle of the twentieth century "created a condition generally favorable towards a scientific study of the future" (Flechtheim 1966b, 71), it also had hampering psychological effects, effects that functioned as "new barriers of resistance against objective and uncompromising forecasting." People were likely to avoid the disturbing reality by retiring into their private lives and neglecting the political life; by concentrating on the past; by hedonistically living only for the moment; or by letting their hopes fully determine their thinking about the future.

However, the futurologist had to forsake these comfortable paths to peace of thought: "[T]he nature of science induces its disciples to continue their search regardless of the outcome" (Flechtheim 1966b, 71). Even if the outcome was devastating, and the prospects for the current human civilization were bad, the futurologist still would have to explore and communicate them neutrally. This also held true for the likely case that when the decline of the civilization had been predicted, the futurologist had no possibility to prevent it from happening. While some humanists might argue that in such situation, ignorance would be a blessing, this was no option to Flechtheim:

> Concealing this truth would equal outright intellectual dishonesty, however. Moreover, even if it were true that complete ignorance is preferable to all knowledge, the fact remains that ours is not the choice between knowing and not knowing. There is no way of returning to a condition of "blessed

---

[3] The challenges posed by attempts to create scientific knowledge about the future have repeatedly provided occasions to question dominant definitions of science and propose fruitful and innovative alternatives (e.g., Helmer and Rescher 1959; Funtowicz and Ravetz 1993; cf. Dayé 2022; Duller and Dayé 2024).

ignorance" – our real and only choice lies between less knowledge and more knowledge. And more knowledge about the days to come may, after all, help dispel some of the worst fears that are plaguing us. (Flechtheim 1966b, 79)

For reasons that might have to do with the publication outlets he had chosen, Flechtheim's early ideas on the future did not receive much scholarly or public attention. Achim Eberspächer (2019, 52) aptly used the term "bottle post" to describe the fate of Flechtheim's ideas on futurology. Coined by Theodor W. Adorno, this metaphor denotes a message written down for generations to come, since the contemporaries are no adequate addressees. A few years after Flechtheim's plea for a new science of the future, thinking about the future had become a broad concern. A major source for this change, as Flechtheim himself acknowledged on several occasions (e.g., Flechtheim 1971, 14), was the publication of the best-selling book *Die Zukunft hat schon begonnen* (1952) by Robert Jungk (1913–1994), published in English as *Tomorrow is Already Here* (1954). This book reignited the public discussion on the future.

Flechtheim and Jungk came from similar geographical and political background. As young men, both had entered a secret organization called *Neu Beginnen* (begin anew) that aimed at overcoming the differences between the German communist party (KPD) and the social-democratic party (SPD). Yet, they did not meet in that capacity, but met in person only later, then becoming close friends (Keßler 2007, 46, 2011, 240; Eberspächer 2019, 129). While Jungk's *Tomorrow is Already Here* certainly led to an increased public engagement with the future, it did hardly match with Flechtheim's ideas for a new science of the future. Rather, it was an example of science journalism that came with the stylistic features of travel literature, resembling rather the writings by Jules Verne and the earlier utopists than Flechtheim's integrative, yet basically scientific approach. Interweaved in a reflection on how new technologies shaped—and endangered—the life on our planet, Jungk reported various episodes form his life in the United States, where he worked as a foreign correspondent for several European newspapers between 1948 and 1957 (Eberspächer 2019, 130). As the most progressed among the nations, the United States exemplified the world's future. And this future was dystopic because of the concessions of some sciences to the wishes of the mighty:

> For in technical science, the atomic industry, biology that encroaches on nature and practical psychology that classifies, men have departed from the

path of truth and allowed themselves to be made instruments of enslavement. In so far as they render aid to inhumanity they endanger the source of every real advance of the fearlessly thinking and feeling human being. (Jungk 1954, 241)

This perspective of Jungk's resulted from his visits to various influential places, among them the nuclear research laboratories in Los Alamos, TX; the US Air Force-sponsored think tank RAND Corporation in Santa Monica, CA, infamous for its analyses of the dawning nuclear war (see below); the Hawthorne facilities, where industrial psychologists had investigated the economic efficiency of caring for "human relations"; or IBM in Endicott, NY, the home of the "thinking machine."

Thus, apart from belonging to a different literary genre, Jungk's book also differed from Flechtheim's in its attempt to function as a warning rather than an invitation to a constructive debate. Some coeval readers understood *Tomorrow is Already Here* to be a testimony of an allegedly deep-seated anti-Americanism on behalf of Jungk's, and this is not too far-fetched. Yet, despite the differences in outlook and approach, Flechtheim and Jungk agreed that thinking about the future was a moral, and thus political obligation of any intellectual. In this, they concurred with Dennis Gabor (1900–1979), a British physicist of Hungarian origin, who was widely known as the inventor of holography, an invention which earned him the 1971 Nobel Prize in Physics. A long-term vision of the human development would be the best guide out of the chaotic and crisis-shaken world people were living in, he claimed in his book *Inventing the Future* (Gabor 1963). Only such a long-term vision would be able to steer social engineering, the second element, after the vision, of the "creative imagination" needed in thinking about the future (Gabor 1963, 19–21).

Gabor (1963, 9) thought that humankind was facing three imminent challenges: destruction by nuclear war, overpopulation, and, somewhat paradoxically, an explosion of leisure.[4] Some years later, Flechtheim (1971, 9) provided a list of now five challenges that futurology had to address: war, hunger and population growth, economic exploitation of humans and lack of democracy, overexploitation of natural resources,

---

[4] Fritz Baade's (1960) book *Der Wettlauf zum Jahre 2000. Paradies oder Selbstvernichtung* [*The race to the year 2000: Paradise or self-desctruction*] treats a similar set of challenges, yet without the objective of establishing a new science, but with an obvious satisfaction with the available forms of knowledge production. This also holds true for lots of other contemporary books, among them Jean Fourastié's (1959) *La civilisation the 1975* [*The civilisation of 1975*].

psychological alienation, and the lack of a new creative *homo humanus*. If humankind did not find solutions to these challenges, they soon would turn into a massive danger for its further existence.

Regardless of how scientific it attempted to be, thinking about the future was therefore always and perforce intrinsically political. Beyond that, given the state of human life on this planet, Flechtheim, Jungk, and Gabor also agreed that it was a moral duty of thinkers to engage in a discourse on the future. In other words, to these writers, it was both epistemologically impossible and morally unjustifiable for futurology to not interfere with its object. The neutral distance to the field that many methodological and philosophical writings promoted as virtue of the scientist was not an option for the futurologist. Quite the opposite: the attempt to avoid an evaluation of possible futures was highly unethical.

Apart from the name of the new science and its moral justification, these early writers also put forth the basic principles that would guide its further activities.[5] True, however, there was a considerable diversity of programmatic approaches, and this diversity was subject to serious critique and re-conception. One crucial outcome of this phase of revisionism was the avoidance of the term futurology and the diffusion of the term futures studies over the last decades of the twentieth century (Paura 2024). The concept of futurology, and their proponents, was seen to suggest that *the future* can be known—something that, for instance, the influential political scientist Bertrand de Jouvenel had fiercely disputed, of whom more is told below. Using the plural also took up de Jouvenel's emphasis on the multiplicity of possible future states. Further, the term studies was attractive as it pointed out the open and, very important, trans-disciplinary character of social scientific work on futures; if the empirical materials of futures studies were present images of the future, then it was important to construct and evaluate such images in close interaction with the people concerned by such images.

The most comprehensive description of this consolidated program of futures studies has been put forth by US sociologist and futures studies scholar Wendell Bell, in the first volume of his all-time classic *Foundations of Futures Studies* (Bell 2003 [1997]). Bell's key assumptions of futures studies are listed in Table 2.1.

---

[5] In Chap. 1, we have already encountered Flechtheim's intriguing conceptualization of the term future.

Table 2.1 Key assumptions of futures studies according to Bell (2003)

Assumption	Remarks
Key assumption 1: The meaning of time	Time is continuous, linear, unidirectional and irreversible. Events occur in time before or after other events and the continuum of time defines the past, present and future (cf. Bell 2003, 140–1)
Key assumption 2: The possible singularity of the future	Not everything that will exist has existed or does exist (cf. Bell 2003, 141)
Key assumption 3: Futures thinking and action	Futures thinking is essential for human action (cf. Bell 2003, 142)
Key assumption 4: The most useful knowledge	In making our way in the world, both individually and collectively, the most useful knowledge is "knowledge of the future" (cf. Bell 2003, 144)
Key assumption 5: Future facts?	The future is nonevidential and cannot be observed; therefore, there are no facts about the future (cf. Bell 2003, 148)
Key assumption 6: An open future	The future is not totally predetermined (cf. Bell 2003, 150)
Key assumption 7: Humans make themselves	To a greater or lesser degree future outcomes can be influenced by individual and collective action (cf. Bell 2003, 154)
Key assumption 8: Interdependence and holism	The interdependence in the world invites a holistic perspective and a transdisciplinary approach, both in the organization of knowledge for decision making and in social action (cf. Bell 2003, 155)
Key assumption 9: Better futures	Some futures are better than others (cf. Bell 2003, 157)

Methods: The American Contribution

Despite the fact that a programmatic consolidation happened only later, it is still safe to say that by the 1950s, there was a theoretical and conceptual framework that formed the foundation for the establishment of a new scientific field. In parallel to these advances on the theoretical side, researchers in the United States began to develop methods and techniques explicitly aimed at studying futures.

The first methods that aimed at producing broad pictures of possible futures and which at the same time attempted to adhere to standards of scientific research were developed in the United States during the 1950s. For the most parts, then, these methods carried as birthmarks the specific political context of their invention, namely, the Cold War and the specific culture of insecurity that characterized this period in global history (Dayé 2020). One place that deserves a specific mention as a hotbed of methodological innovation in this regard was the RAND Corporation, a think tank that emerged out of a collaboration project between the US Air Force and Douglas Aircraft Company begun in 1947 (Smith 1966; Hounshell 1997; Collins 2002). The objective of RAND was to continue lines of Research ANd Development that had proven to be successful during World War II—hence the name.

In the first decades of its existence, RAND management gave its researchers a great amount of freedom to define and select research projects. As a consequence, the researchers found sufficient resources to engage in the development of new methods and techniques and to experiment with them in a playful, yet dedicated manner. Many influential research techniques originated at RAND during the 1950s, among them systems analysis, the methodology informing the Planning, Programming, and Budgeting System (PPBS) introduced to US federal government institutions during the 1960s (Jardini 2000; Levien 2000; Duller 2016; Rindzevičiūtė 2019). Also, RAND was important in furthering the development of mathematical game theory (Mirowski 1992, 1999, 2002; Leonard 2010; Erickson 2015).

For futures studies, three methodological innovations proved to be of highest relevance: scenario analysis created by Herman Kahn, the Delphi method invented by Olaf Helmer and Norman C. Dalkey, and political gaming developed by Herbert Goldhamer, Hans Speier, and Paul Kecskemeti. To begin with, the term scenarios was reportedly introduced at RAND by Leo Rosten (1980–1997), a writer who had become involved with RAND in the early years of the organization's existence. During the war effort, Rosten had been a deputy director the Office of War Information (OWI), and personal friendships to several economists made him a repeatedly sought consultant when RAND began to set up its Social Science and Economics Divisions. At that time, however, Rosten was already mainly interested in writing film scripts for Hollywood. At RAND, the term became used for a text that "tells what happened and describes the environment in which it happened" (DeWeerd 1967, 2). Scenarios are thus narrative descriptions of situations that are not yet real. As such, they can be used for planning and evaluating situations that cannot be directly observed. The more comprehensive such a scenario, the better it triggers the imagination necessary to explore the consequences of the events described in it. On the other hand, the closer the scenario to currently conceivable futures (e.g., by including predictions of certain aspects that allow for extrapolation), the more stable the results of the ensuing analysis. The first published analyses of nuclear war scenarios were included in Herman Kahn's book *On Thermonuclear War* (Kahn 1961), which caused a considerable outburst in public media, as it seriously explored various options for human survival in the devastations of an all-out nuclear war between the United States and the Soviet Union (Ghamari-Tabrizi 2005; Dayé 2020, chap. 2). Kahn continued to use scenario analysis in his later works, for example, in his book, co-written with Anthony Wiener on *The Year 2000* (Kahn and Wiener 1967).

Delphi, on the other hand, was invented by Olaf Helmer (1910–2011) and Norman C. Dalkey (1915–2003), who were both members of RAND's Mathematics Division. Delphi asks experts to provide estimations, and does so repeatedly, feeding back various kinds of information between the interrogation phases. The first Delphi study, conducted in the first half of 1951, aimed at providing stable expert estimations of "the selection, from the viewpoint of a Soviet strategic planner, of an optimal U. S. industrial target system" as well as "of the number of A-bombs required to reduce munitions output by a prescribed amount" (Dalkey and Helmer 1963, 458). After each round of interrogation, the experts were informed, in an anonymized way, of the estimates of the other participating experts and invited to reconsider their original estimations. At times, additional information was also disseminated (e.g., production data). This led to a convergence of the individual figures: estimates that initially were quite dispersed came closer to each other over time, and the median value of them was then taken to be a stable and consensual group estimate (Dayé 2018).

Better known than this early Delphi study, and sometimes erroneously referred to as the first Delphi, is the long-range forecasting study that Helmer and Theodore J. Gordon (1930–2024), a young engineer and soon-to-be renowned futurist, published in 1964. The study convened a panel of experts and asked them to provide their estimations on six areas of interest: (1) scientific breakthroughs; (2) population control; (3) automation; (4) space progress; (5) war prevention; and (6) weapon systems (Gordon and Helmer 1964, 2). The experts remain unnamed, with the notable exception of Dennis Gabor and Bertrand de Jouvenel, who are thanked by name (Gordon and Helmer 1964, ix). Data collection was facilitated via mail, with questionnaires being sent out roughly every second month between June 1963 and January 1964. Consolidated results concerned the control and regional manipulation of weather, which experts estimated to be possible around 1990 (median; quartiles: 1987 and 2000); that robots would take care of the disposal of garbage and other chores in the household by 1988 (median; quartiles: 1980 and 1996); and a permanent base on the moon accommodating ten persons by 1982 (median; quartiles: 1982 and 1982 [!]).

Political gaming, on the other hand, was developed by members of RAND's Social Science Division in 1954, among them Herbert Goldhamer (1907–1977), Hans Speier (1905–1990), and Paul Kecskemeti (1901–1980). The game designed mainly by Herbert Goldhamer proposed to invite a selected group of people with proven expertise in foreign policy to RAND for about half a week. In groups, these experts would then represent selected national governments—the United States, the Soviet Union, and "other governments." The groups were allowed to make any move they could reasonably justify as a plausible action or reaction of the government they represented. The moves were checked for plausibility by a committee of referees (or umpires), who also were in charge of facilitating the communication process, collecting the moves, and generate a new state of play synthesizing the different moves. No further rules were devised before the start of the game.

Between February 1955 and April 1956, four such political games were played at RAND. They started from varying scenarios, and aimed to assess the possible actions and reactions of the represented political actors. However, summarizing RAND's experiments with political games, Speier and Goldhamer suggested not to pursue this approach any further at RAND, mainly because of a missing balance between the required effort and the stability of the results obtained. Political gaming was then further developed at other places, most notably by a group led by Lincoln P. Bloomfield

(1920–2013) at MIT (Bloomfield and Padelford 1959; Bloomfield 1960; Barringer and Whaley 1965; Bloomfield and Whaley 1965).

From these early examples, we can draw a series of lessons on particular characteristics of methodological approaches in futures studies. First, a core instrument of futures studies are scenarios. Scenarios can come in different shapes, ranging from narrative to tabular form (Peperhove et al. 2018), but one key aspect of scenarios—and of narrative scenarios in particular—is that they are supposed to trigger the imagination of the reader while at the same time showing certain links to the present reality. Second, experts are an utterly important source of empirical data in futures studies. Both Delphi and political gaming procedures consist of interacting with experts, and scenario analyses also often draw on expert knowledge. Third, futures studies cover a range of possible questions. In its classic form, Delphi asked how the future will look like. Scenario analysis and the form of gaming just described, on the other hand, are more concerned with asking what consequences a particular future event or situation will have. Another technique developed a decade later by Robert Jungk, the Future Workshop (Jungk and Müllert 1983), was more concerned with asking what kind of future do we want.

Out of these first approaches developed at RAND thus emerged a wealth of different methods and techniques specifically developed for futures studies that allowed its practitioners to address the relevant questions related to the future. While most of them show considerable similarity to research methods used in other social sciences, in particular in sociology, others are further away from the academic canon and closer to techniques of group moderation or visioneering used in management. This allows futures studies practitioners to offer their services to a broad variety of clients, from private to public, and offer the results in a variety of ways, from openly accessible publication in scientific outlets to proprietary, unpublished reports.

The Institutionalization of Futures Studies: Futuribles and the World Futures Studies Federation

The first organization dedicated specifically to futures studies presumably had been the Centre d'études prospective founded in 1958 by philosopher Gaston Berger (1896–1960). However, after the untimely death of its founder, the Centre soon ceased to produce noteworthy output (H. de Jouvenel 2019, 9). In the same year that Berger died, French political scientist Bertrand de Jouvenel (1903–1987) founded the Futuribles International Committee. A self-declared conservative, De Jouvenel also had been a founding member of the Mont Pélerin Society. Based on relations established there, and with considerable funding by the Ford Foundation, the committee brought together an international group of renowned intellectuals to indulge in future thinking along a wide range of topics. When Ford's financial support ended in late 1965, de Jouvenel pondered a new organizational form, and finally founded the not-for-profit association Futuribles International Association in 1967, which exists until today. De Jouvenel was the association's first president, but did not stay in office for long. Later, his son Hugues de Jouvenel (1946–) steered the organization. Today, Futuribles is directed by Hugues's son (and Bertrand's grandson), François de Jouvenel.

The word futuribles was Jouvenel's invention. He used it, partly, as a contrast to the term "prospective" used by Berger: De Jouvenel was convinced that in a strict sense, humans can't know anything about the future. In a talk held in 1964 at the RAND Corporation in which he described the Futuribles committee, de Jouvenel put it straightforward: "*[T]here can be no science of the future. The future is not the realm of the true or false but the realm of possibles*" (B. de Jouvenel 1965, 2; emphases in original). Being unable to grasp with certainty the things which will be, our thinking about the future necessarily amounts to a speculative pondering of possible futures—hence, of futuribles. Possible futures could be defined as futuribles if the ways by which they might emerge from the present state of affairs were imaginable and plausible. "For example, aviation was seen as a possible already in ancient times, but it became a futurible only when certain new facts made its development conceivable" (B. de Jouvenel 1967, 18). Bertrand de Jouvenel also emphasized that the word should be used in the plural form, paving, in a sense, the way for the field's currently preferred name "futures studies."

The Futuribles committee had commissioned and published a series of essays on the future, apparently without pressuring the authors into a specific theoretical direction but giving them leeway to speculate about the things to come. It also had organized a series of international conferences, held annually in the years from 1962 to 1965 in Geneva, Paris, New Haven (CT), and again Paris. These conferences were important events in the formation of futures studies, as they helped establish and maintain an international discursive space. Hugues de Jouvenel remembers the participation of such important figures as Daniel Bell, Herman Kahn, and Hasan Ozbeckhan (H. de Jouvenel 2019, 11).

These activities also formed the context in which Bertrand de Jouvenel elaborated and polished his own theoretical position on the study of the future, which he laid down in a book called *L'art de conjecture* published in 1964 and explained in a series of lectures in the United States. An English translation of *The Art of Conjecture* appeared in 1967, and was widely received—and still is (see Chap. 4). Apparently, de Jouvenel was perceived as a model of how a theoretical program could be successfully entangled with institutional entrepreneurship in the area of futures studies. He proved that the project of doing futures studies would provide sufficient leverage to carry a research organization, and this inspired many people worldwide. Just to take examples of former RAND employees: Herman Kahn, who had left RAND soon after the publication of *On Thermonuclear War* to found the Hudson Institute as an independent think tank, transformed from a nuclear strategist into a full-fledged futurist. And together with the computer engineer Paul Baran and the already mentioned Theodore Gordon, Olaf Helmer left RAND in 1968 to found the Institute for the Future (IFTF). Both organizations are still in operation today.

Continuing the networking mission of the earlier international committee, Futuribles International Association also was part of the group that founded, in 1973, the World Futures Studies Federation (WFSF). Discussions on the need to establish an additional international scholarly association that did not emphasize a particular theoretical approach like futuribles had begun during the Mankind 2000 conference organized by Robert Jungk and Johan Galtung in Oslo (1967), and were continued over two further conferences, in Kyoto (1970) and Bucharest (1972). A person of particular importance at this juncture was the Russian historian Igor Bestuzhev-Lada (1927–2015), who was a key figure in Soviet "prognostics" and a regular participant in UNESCO activities (Bestuzhev-Lada 1971, 1992; on the broader context, see Rindzevičiūtė 2016; Steinmüller 2023). Building on this social and intellectual capital, the group turned to de Jouvenel and leading members of Futuribles International. Together, they could secure the support of UNESCO, which was instrumental for the official creation of the WFSF (Masini 2005).

The WFSF was initially housed in the premises of the Maison Internationale Futuribles, and de Jouvenel became its founding president. Soon after, Johan Galtung took over. As Sardar (2013, 39) notes, the name was intended to contrast clearly to the US-based World Future Society, which was seen by the protagonists to be more a business enterprise than a scientific association. Hence, the term "federation" and also the plural form "futures" to "emphasize plurality and alternatives" (Sardar 2013, 39).

The focus on these developments in the international scenery is of course not meant to suggest that there were no steps of establishments at the national level. Indeed, there were, as the above-mentioned installments of the Hudson Institution, the Institute for the Future, the World Future Society, and also the founding of the Hawaii Research Center for Futures Studies by Jim Dator in 1971 testify. Yet, the conception of futures studies that all these different organizations epitomized was one that emphasized thinking with uncertainties, thinking in alternatives, and thinking internationally.

Conclusion: Futures Studies and Sociology

UNESCO had been a constant source of support for the institutionalization at the international level not just of futures studies (cf. Paura 2024) but of futures thinking more generally. It had supported the foundation of the International Sociological Association (ISA) in 1949 (Platt 1998, 16), which, in turn, saw the installment of a Research Committee dedicated to studies of the future in 1971. Interestingly, however, no bipartite institutionalization could be observed in the early 1970s. By and large, the persons acting as leaders of the new organizations were the same, and the intent to allow for a better coordination between futures studies and sociology was explicitly addressed. Within the ISA, Bestuzhev-Lada had acted as chairman of the working group that paved the way for the proposal of a new Research Committee dedicated to "Social Forecasting and Long-Term Planning" (ISA RC07), and in 1972 accepted to be co-president of RC07 after the formal acceptance of the proposal—the other co-president being de Jouvenel. Two years later, the name of the RC was changed to "Sociological Problems of Futures Research." Toward the end of the 1970s, Eleonora Masini (1928–2022) was elected member of the board, who at that time also acted as the General Secretary of the WFSF before becoming the Federation's president in 1981. This was seen as an advantage as it offered the possibility "to coordinate more effectively their [i.e., the two organizations] working efforts."[6]

But despite these attempts to have futures studies and sociology join forces, the two fields drifted away from each other. While this is addressed more explicitly in the empirical studies presented in later chapters, here is the place to reflect on possible historical roots for the bipartite

---

[6] See ISA Bulletin 20, Summer 1982, p. 5–6; available online at https://www.isa-sociology.org/uploads/files/isa-bulletin29.pdf, last visited 24 February 2025.

institutionalization of futures thinking in the social sciences. Why is it that there is a body of thinking in sociology that engages in futures thinking, but shows no systematic reception of debates happening in futures studies? And why is it that futures studies practitioners, with notable exceptions, refrain from integrating sociological theories and viewpoints into their arguments?

One answer may start with understanding that it is not a lack of mutual understanding of the urgency of social scientific futures thinking that separates the two fields. The problem arose with the tensions such futures thinking has with standard philosophy of science. Yet, the problem itself is not philosophical—there are alternative approaches to thinking of science that can accommodate the problems mentioned in the opening paragraphs of this chapter. The problem is one of social acknowledgment. Sociology has long been fighting for its place as a legitimate social science, and throughout the twentieth century, it found it risky to engage with approaches, literatures, and fields that may undermine its own status—social reputations are sticky, and they spread. Futures studies, on the other hand, cherished the proximity to decision-makers, as it allowed them to have their voices heard. The lack of academic integration made large parts of futures studies dependent on clients other than students—they reconfigured themselves as market actors, producing shiny publications on megatrends for a well-paying audience.

Admittedly, this analysis is sketchy, but it will be pursued in more detail in later parts of the book. Then, it will also be able to draw on theoretically richer concepts, which are introduced in the next chapter.

REFERENCES

Baade, Fritz. 1960. *Der Wettlauf zum Jahre 2000. Paradies oder Selbstvernichtung.* Oldenburg, Hamburg: Gerhard Stalling.

Barringer, Richard E., and Barton Whaley. 1965. The M.I.T. Political-Military Gaming Experience. *Orbis* IX:437–458.

Bell, Wendell. 2003. *Foundations of Futures Studies. Volume 1: History, Purposes, and Knowledge.* 2nd ed. Human Science for a New Era 1. New Brunswick, NJ: Transaction Publishers.

Bestuzhev-Lada, Igor V. 1971. A Soviet Scientist Looks at Futurology. *The UNESCO Courier* 24:22–27.

Bestuzhev-Lada, Igor V. 1992. A Short History of Forecasting in the USSR, 1927–1990. *Technological Forecasting and Social Change* 41:341–348. https://doi.org/10.1016/0040-1625(92)90030-W.

Bloomfield, Lincoln P. 1960. Political Gaming. *United States Naval Institute Proceedings* 86:57–64.
Bloomfield, Lincoln P., and Norman J. Padelford. 1959. Teaching Note: Three Experiments in Political Gaming. *The American Political Science Review* 53:1105–1115.
Bloomfield, Lincoln P., and Barton Whaley. 1965. The Political-Military Exercise. *Orbis* VIII:854–870.
Collins, Martin J. 2002. *Cold War Laboratory: RAND, the Air Force, and the American State, 1945–1950.* Washington, London: Smithsonian University Press.
Dalkey, Norman C., and Olaf Helmer. 1963. An Experimental Application of the Delphi Method to the Use of Experts. *Management Science* 9:458–467.
Dayé, Christian. 2018. How to Train Your Oracle: The Delphi Method and Its Turbulent Youth in Operations Research and the Policy Sciences. *Social Studies of Science* 48:846–868. https://doi.org/10.1177/0306312718798497.
Dayé, Christian. 2020. *Experts, Social Scientists, and Techniques of Prognosis in Cold War America.* Cham, CH: Palgrave Macmillan.
Dayé, Christian. 2022. On the Icy Slopes of Expertise: How a Cold War-Era Solution to the Problem of Expert Opinion in Science Might Transform the Epistemology of Simulation. *Futures* 142:103012. https://doi.org/10.1016/j.futures.2022.103012.
DeWeerd, Harvey A. 1967. *Political-Military Scenarios. P-3535.* Santa Monica (CA): The RAND Corporation.
Duller, Matthias. 2016. Internationalization of Cold War Systems Analysis: RAND, IIASA and the Institutional Reasons for Methodological Change. *History of the Human Sciences* 29:172–190. https://doi.org/10.1177/0952695116667882.
Duller, Matthias, and Christian Dayé. 2024. Globalisierte Gültigkeit: Internationale Politikanalyse am IIASA, 1972–1992. In *Organisationsformen der Erkenntnisgewinnung: Organisatorische Gestaltung und Wissensproduktion in der außeruniversitären Forschung*, ed. Rupert Pichler and Thomas Heinze, 327–345. Wiesbaden: Springer Fachmedien. https://doi.org/10.1007/978-3-658-44331-3_15.
Eberspächer, Achim. 2019. *Das Projekt Futurologie: Über Zukunft und Fortschritt in der Bundesrepublik 1952–1982.* Leiden, Boston: Brill Schöningh.
Erickson, Paul. 2015. *The World the Game Theorists Made.* Chicago, London: The University of Chicago Press.
Eyal, Gil. 2019. Trans-science as a Vocation. *Journal of Classical Sociology* 19:254–274. https://doi.org/10.1177/1468795X19851377.
Flechtheim, Ossip K. 1943. Toynbee and the Webers. *Phylon (1940-1956)* 4:248–264. https://doi.org/10.2307/271437.

Flechtheim, Ossip K. 1966a. Teaching the Future. In *History and Futurology. With a foreword by Robert Jungk*, 63–68. Meisenheim am Glan: Anton Hain.
Flechtheim, Ossip K. 1966b. Futurology - The New Science of Probability? In *History and Futurology. With a foreword by Robert Jungk*, 69–80. Meisenheim am Glan: Anton Hain.
Flechtheim, Ossip K. 1968. *Futurologie - Möglichkeiten und Grenzen*. Projekte und Modelle 3. Frankfurt am Main, Berlin: Edition Voltaire.
Flechtheim, Ossip K. 1969. Is Futurology the Answer to the Challenge of the Future? In *Mankind 2000*, ed. Robert Jungk and Johan Galtung, 264–269. Oslo: Universitetsforlaget.
Flechtheim, Ossip K. 1971. *Futurologie. Der Kampf um die Zukunft*. 2. Auflage. Köln: Verlag Wissenschaft und Politik.
Fourastié, Jean. 1959. *La civilization de 1975*. Paris: Presses universitaires de France.
Funtowicz, Silvio O., and Jerome R. Ravetz. 1993. Science for the Post-normal Age. *Futures* 25:739–755. https://doi.org/10.1016/0016-3287(93)90022-L.
Gabor, Dennis. 1963. *Inventing the future*. London: Secker and Warburg.
Ghamari-Tabrizi, Sharon. 2005. *The Worlds of Herman Kahn. The Intuitive Science of Thermonuclear War*. Cambridge (MA), London: Harvard University Press.
Gordon, Theodore J., and Olaf Helmer. 1964. *Report on a Long-Range Forecasting Study*. P-2982. Santa Monica (CA): The RAND Corporation.
Helmer, Olaf, and Nicholas Rescher. 1959. On the Epistemology of the Inexact Sciences. *Management Science* 6:25–52.
Hempel, Carl G., and Paul Oppenheim. 1945. A Definition of "Degree of Confirmation". *Philosophy of Science* 12:98–115.
Hounshell, David. 1997. The Cold War, RAND, and the Generation of Knowledge, 1946-1962. *Historical Studies in the Physical and Biological Sciences* 27:237–267.
Jardini, David. 2000. Out of the Blue Yonder: The Transfer of Systems Thinking from the Pentagon to the Great Society, 1961-1965. In *Systems, Experts, and Computers: The Systems Approach in Management and Engineering, World War II and After*, ed. Agatha C. Hughes and Thomas P. Hughes, 311–358. Cambridge (MA), London: The MIT Press.
Jouvenel, Bertrand de. 1965. *Futuribles*. P-3034. Santa Monica (CA): The RAND Corporation.
Jouvenel, Bertrand de. 1967. *The Art of Conjecture*. New York: Basic Books.
Jouvenel, Hugues de. 2019. Futuribles: Origins, Philosophy, and Practices—Anticipation for Action. *World Futures Review* 11:8–18. https://doi.org/10.1177/1946756718777490.
Jungk, Robert. 1952. *Die Zukunft hat schon begonnen. Amerikas Allmacht und Ohnmacht*. Bern, Stuttgart: Alfred Scherz.
Jungk, Robert. 1954. *Tomorrow is Already Here*. Simon and Schuster.

Jungk, Robert, and Norbert R. Müllert. 1983. *Zukunftswerkstätten. Wege zur Wiederbelebung der Demokratie*. München: Goldmann.

Kahn, Herman. 1961. On Thermonuclear War. In *Three Lectures and Several Suggestions. Second Edition with Index*. Princeton (NJ): Princeton University Press.

Kahn, Herman, and Anthony J. Wiener. 1967. *The Year 2000: A Framework for Speculation on the Next Thirty-three Years*. Macmillan.

Keßler, Mario. 2007. *Ossip K. Flechtheim: politischer Wissenschaftler und Zukunftsdenker (1909–1998)*. Köln: Böhlau.

Keßler, Mario. 2011. Zur Futurologie von Ossip K. Flechtheim. In *Macht und Geist im Kalten Krieg*, ed. Bernd Greiner, Tim B. Müller, and Claudia Weber, 239–257. Hamburg: Hamburger Edition.

Leonard, Robert J. 2010. *Von Neumann, Morgenstern, and the Creation of Game Theory: From Chess to Social Science, 1900–1960*. Cambridge, New York etc.: Cambridge University Press.

Levien, Roger E. 2000. RAND, IIASA, and the Conduct of Systems Analysis. In *Systems, Experts, and Computers. The Systems Approach in Management and Engineering, World War II and After*, ed. Agatha C. Hughes and Thomas P. Hughes, 433–462. Cambridge (Mass.), London: The MIT Press.

Masini, Eleonora Barbieri. 2005. Reflections on World Futures Studies Federation. *Futures* 37:361–369. https://doi.org/10.1016/j.futures.2004.10.001.

Merton, Robert K. 1948. The Self-Fulfilling Prophecy. *The Antioch Review* 8:193–210.

Mirowski, Philip. 1992. What Were von Neumann and Morgenstern Trying to Accomplish? In *Toward a History of Game Theory. Annual Supplement to History of Political Economy*, ed. E. Roy Weintraub, vol. 24, 113–147. Durham, London: Duke University Press.

Mirowski, Philip. 1999. Cyborg Agonistes. *Social Studies of Science* 29:685–718.

Mirowski, Philip. 2002. *Machine Dreams: Economics Becomes a Cyborg Science*. Cambridge, UK, New York: Cambridge University Press.

Neumann, Franz. 1942. *Behemoth: The Structure and Practice of National Socialism, 1933–1944*. Oxford, New York: Oxford University Press.

Paura, Roberto. 2024. About the history of Futures Studies. In *Handbook of Futures Studies*, ed. Roberto Poli, 10–24. Cheltenham, UK, Northampton, MA: Edward Elgar.

Peperhove, Roman, Karlheinz Steinmüller, and Hans-Liudger Dienel. 2018. *Envisioning Uncertain Futures: Scenarios as a Tool in Security, Privacy and Mobility Research*. 1st ed. Springer VS: Zukunft Und Forschung.

Platt, Jennifer. 1998. *A Brief History of the ISA*. Québec: The International Sociological Association.

Reichmann, Werner. 2018. *Wirtschaftsprognosen. Eine Soziologie des Wissens über die ökonomische Zukunft*. Frankfurt am Main, New York: Campus.

Rindzevičiūtė, Eglė. 2016. A Struggle for the Soviet Future: The Birth of Scientific Forecasting in the Soviet Union. *Slavic Review* 75:52–76. https://doi.org/10.5612/slavicreview.75.1.52.

Rindzevičiūtė, Eglė. 2019. Systems Analysis as Infrastructural Knowledge: Scientific Expertise and Dissensus under State Socialism. In *Economic Knowledge in Socialism, 1945-89*, ed. Till Düppe and Ivan Boldyrev, 204–227. Annual Supplement to Volume 51, History of Political Economy. Durham, London: Duke University Press.

Sardar, Ziauddin. 2013. *Future: All that Matters*. London: Hodder & Stoughton.

Smith, Bruce L. R. 1966. *The RAND Corporation. Case Study of a Nonprofit Advisory Corporation*. Cambridge (MA): Harvard University Press.

Steinmüller, Karlheinz. 2023. The Rise and Decline of Prognostics. Futures Studies, Ideology and the Sociology of Knowledge in the German Democratic Republic. *The American Sociologist*. 55:142. https://doi.org/10.1007/s12108-023-09570-7.

Weinberg, Alvin M. 1972. Science and Trans-Science. *Minerva* 10:209–222.

CHAPTER 3

The Sociology of Scientific Collectives: A Conceptual Overview

Abstract This chapter presents different approaches to describe the shape and characteristics of groups and collectives in the sciences, the humanities, and the arts. The conceptualizations introduced are thought collective and thought style (L. Fleck); academic tribes and territories (T. Becher, P. Trowler); epistemic culture (K. Knorr Cetina); the scientific community (W. Hagstrom); the invisible college (D. Crane); the scientific school (E. Tiryakian); the collaborative circle (M. Farrell); the epistemic community (P. Haas); and the scientific/intellectual movement (S. Frickel & N. Gross). These considerations pave the way for the theoretical framework and the related research design used in the studies described in this book.

Keywords Scientific schools • Thought collectives • Thought styles • Epistemic community • Collaborative circles

INTRODUCTION

Futures thinking has seen a bipartite institutionalization in the social sciences. With futures studies on the one hand and the sociology of the future on the other, there are apparently two knowledge collectives that concern themselves with a similar task, namely, the exploration of *the future* as a broad category. While the historical roots of this bipartite

© The Author(s), under exclusive license to Springer Nature Switzerland AG 2025
C. Dayé, *Futures Thinking*,
https://doi.org/10.1007/978-3-031-91941-1_3

institutionalization have been described in the previous chapter, this chapter now shifts the focus to our understanding of knowledge collectives as social forms.

Over the centuries, scholars have proposed various terms and metaphors to describe science as a social form. Of these, the Republic of Letters appears to be the oldest term: it can be traced back to an exchange of letters between two Italian scholars in the early fifteenth century.[1] With the emergence of sociology, and in particular the sociology of science, conceptualizations of scientific collectives have proliferated.

In order to contextualize the theoretical framework and research design introduced in Chap. 4, this chapter presents different approaches to describe the shape and characteristics of groups and collectives in the sciences, the humanities, and the arts. These options are ordered according to their respective analytical emphases (see Table 3.1). A first category of concepts focuses on the relations between the social form of a knowledge collective and the notion of knowledge that it entertains (respectively, the kind of knowledge it produces). In this category, this chapter discusses thought collective and thought style (L. Fleck); academic tribes and territories (T. Becher, P. Trowler); and epistemic culture (K. Knorr Cetina).

Table 3.1 Concepts of scientific collectives according to their analytical foci

Analytical focus	Concepts
Relations between social form/practices and knowledge	• Thought collective and thought style (L. Fleck) • Academic tribes and territories (T. Becher, P. Trowler) • Epistemic culture (K. Knorr Cetina)
Actor-based communication networks	• The scientific community (W. Hagstrom) • The invisible college (D. Crane)
Group structures and dynamics	• The scientific school (E. Tiryakian) • The collaborative circle (M. Farrell)
Science–policy nexus	• The epistemic community (P. Haas) • The scientific/intellectual movement (S. Frickel and N. Gross)

---

[1] Cf. Fabien Simon, "The Republic of Letters (seventeenth-eighteenth centuries)," *Encyclopédie d'histoire numérique de l'Europe* [online], ISSN 2677-6588, published on 22/06/2020, consulted on 17/02/2025. Permalink: https://ehne.fr/en/node/12466

A second category approached the description of social forms by tracing networks of communication between members of the knowledge collective. The scientific community (W. Hagstrom) and the invisible college (D. Crane) fall in this category. A third group of concepts has taken inspiration from small group research and explored the social and psychological dynamics at play in knowledge collectives (of a certain size). Here, the scientific school (E. Tiryakian) and the collaborative circle (M. Farrell) are discussed as examples. Finally, a fourth group of concepts, including the epistemic community (P. Haas) and the scientific/intellectual movement (S. Frickel & N. Gross), emphasized relations between science and policy.

Each of these terms has initially been conceptualized for a particular research interest. Therefore, certain theoretical and methodological ideas are woven into each of these terms, which need to be known if one wants to exploit their full analytical potential and prevent misunderstandings. The following sections focus on these inherent assumptions and provide examples of how they emphasize particular aspects and mechanisms when used in analysis. The conceptualizations are discussed in roughly chronological order.

Relations Between Social Form and Knowledge

The search for mutual relations between the social shape of a knowledge collective and the tacit and explicit premises of its notion of knowledge has been the core project of the sociology of knowledge since its earliest conceptions. Michel Foucault famously argued that the relations between words and things, *les mots et les choses*, create order, while at the same time hiding this capacity from the eyes of the observer by making order somehow naturally given. "The fundamental codes of a culture—those governing its language, its schemas of perception, its exchanges, its techniques, its values, the hierarchy of its practices—establish for every man, from the very first, the empirical orders with which he will be dealing and within which he will be at home" (Foucault 2002, xxii). Outside of this order, we have no words, and where we have no words, we cannot see things. Obviously, by empirical orders, Foucault also means the social organization of the knowledge collective, and its shape.

While not agreeing with everything that Foucault has said, sociologists of knowledge still hold to their task of identifying similarities, or affinities, or relations, between the social shape of a community and its concept of knowledge. Over the last decades, some of the most influential conceptualizations to capture the relations between social form and knowledge were *thought collective and thought style* introduced by Ludwik Fleck, *academic tribes and territories* as initially described by Tony Becher, and *epistemic cultures* as explored by Karin Knorr Cetina.

Thought Collectives and Thought Styles

Not surprisingly, the terms used to capture the relations between social form and knowledge very often come in the form of two-word combinations. One of the popular combinations is the term pair *thought collective* and *thought style*. It was coined by Ludwik Fleck in his book *Genesis and Development of a Scientific Fact* (Fleck 1979), first published in 1935 as *Entstehung und Entwicklung einer wissenschaftlichen Tatsache*, which has since become a classic. The history of this book is itself the subject of historical work. Suffice it to say that a wider readership first became interested in it when Thomas S. Kuhn mentioned it in 1962 in the preface of his monograph *The Structure of Scientific Revolutions* (Kuhn 1970, vi–vii)—a book that is presented in more detail in the section on the scientific community.

For Fleck, the thought collective is the "community of persons mutually exchanging ideas or maintaining intellectual interaction" that "provides the special 'carrier' for the historical development of any field of thought, as well as for the given stock of knowledge and level of culture. This we have designated thought style" (Fleck 1979, 39). The thought style determines what is known and how it is known. Defined as "directed perception, with corresponding mental and objective assimilation of what has been so perceived" (Fleck 1979, 99), the thought style determines how to think correctly and what is considered to be true. It impacts the individual in the form of unquestioned principles and factual, albeit unconscious, thinking constraints. Cognition is thus not the result of individual but of social activity. Just as the sentence "Town A is situated to the left of town B" must be specified by adding "to someone standing on the road between towns A and B while facing north" in order to be informative, the statement "Someone recognizes something" also requires the supplement "in a particular thought style, in a particular thought collective" (Fleck 1979, 38–39). Not surprisingly, Fleck's book is today regarded as a key work of constructivism (cf. Egloff 2011).

Individuals can belong to several thought collectives, for example, when physicists are also devout members of a religious community.

However, the thinking styles of these collectives are fundamentally incompatible with each other. This also applies when people from different thought collectives meet. "One can never say that the same thought is true for A and false for B. If A and B belong to the same thought collective, the thought will be either true or false for both. But if they belong to different thought collectives, it will just *not* be *the same* thought! It must be unclear to, or be understood differently by, one of them" (Fleck 1979, 100).

Fleck's treatise contains some explanations on how thought collectives differentiate themselves on the basis of their thinking styles. In the field of science, he distinguishes between different types of thought collectives, each with different concepts of knowledge: popular science, journal science, vademecum science, and textbook science (Fleck 1979, 112ff). Popular science, for example, does not follow the principle of strict proof like journal science, but is committed to simplification and valuation. Beyond such rudimentary remarks, Fleck does not concern himself with the social structure of thought collectives. For him, the concept of the thought collective, "as we use it to investigate the social conditioning of thinking, is not to be understood as a fixed group or social class. It is functional, as it were, rather than substantial, and may be compared to the concept of field of force in physics" (Fleck 1979, 102). His primary interest is directed toward the development of a sociological approach to the theory of knowledge and science, one that conceptualizes an interrelation between knowledge, the collective of the knowers, and their social epistemology.

To the student of the social organization of the sciences, Fleck's concept of thought collective can be useful in situations where two scientific collectives are creating knowledge about an object that are identical to laypeople, but without being able to draw on the results of each other. As to the scientists, the object is informed by their respective thought styles, they aren't identical to each other. For instance, we could talk about thought collectives if "the future" in futures studies would be totally incomprehensible to a sociologist (of the future). In anticipation of what will become clear in later chapters, we can, however, ascertain that this is not the case.

Interestingly, though, in her German publications, historian Elke Seefried (2014, 2015a) used the term pair to describe three dominant approaches in futures studies.[2] The first, *empirical and positivistic* thought

---

[2] In her English publications, Seefried replaced the term "Denkstil" used in from her German publications (Seefried 2015a, 2015b) with the term "approaches" (Seefried 2014).

style, was characterized by the belief that technology was the major factor in shaping the futures. Informed by a positivist conception of science, proponents of this approach were convinced that they could provide reasonable and scientifically bolstered findings about the future, that these findings in themselves were value-neutral, and that they could (and should) be used be decision-makers in government, business, and the military.

The second approach, which Seefried call the *normative and ontological* thought style, was taken by individuals who were more eager to acknowledge that foreknowledge necessarily entails an aspect of morality and values. They were seeking to develop ideas about the "good" future and quite certain that technology should remain a tool of civilization, not its driver. Their understanding of the channels between ideas and political power, however, was elitist. Thinking about the future was not an issue of democratic deliberation, but the craft of the trained and seasoned thinker. This was the main difference to the third approach, the *critical and emancipatory* thought style, which found that from the fundamental moral nature of future thinking resulted the need to ensure its happening in democratic settings. The proponents of this thought style were critical of power inequalities, and called for the participation of citizens in all thinking and deciding about the future.

Seefried's analysis focuses on the history of futures studies during the 1960s and 1970s, yet traces of these approaches—or thought styles—can be found today as well, even at the level of certain methodologies used in futures studies. For instance, standard Delphi surveys are rooted in the positivist philosophy of science characteristic of the first approach (Tolon 2012; Dayé 2018), whereas policy games still reflect their origin in an elitist understanding of political processes (Bessner 2018); future workshops, as conceived of by Robert Jungk, clearly belong to the third approach described by Seefried. Further, the public image that futures studies scholars like to create for themselves also appear to differ accordingly.

Academic Tribes and Territories

Another term pair proposed to capture the relations between the social shape of a knowledge collective and its concept of knowledge has been academic tribes and territories. At the time when Tony Becher (1989)

The analysis and the threefold scheme presented in these publications, however, are identical, which is why it is justified to use, for the sake of clarity, the term "thought style" in this chapter.

published the first edition of his book, *Academic Tribes and Territories*, he made use of the colloquial metaphor of the academic tribe, well aware of the fact that the notion of tribe had been discredited within anthropology (e.g., by Fried 1966, 1975). To Becher, disciplines as well as specialized fields within disciplines can be defined as academic tribes. However, he not only took an interest in analyzing the social structure of such tribes but also in exploring how these structures interact with the tribe's territory, that is, the area of knowledge which they claim to possess. The starting point is the conviction that "the ways in which particular groups of academics organize their professional lives are related in important ways to the intellectual tasks on which they are engaged" (Becher and Trowler 2001, 23). The tribe's culture, its set of norms, and its internal organization are understood as being intrinsically related to the nature and quality of their territory, that is, their realm of knowledge claims.

Potentially misleading, the concept of discipline encompasses both a knowledge component—the territory—and a social component—the tribe. However, if this link is severed for analytical purposes, both dimensions, the epistemic and the sociological dimension, can be broken down further. On the epistemic dimension, disciplines or specialties can be distinguished according to whether they produce (I) hard or soft knowledge and (II) pure or applied knowledge. On the sociological dimension, a distinction can be made as to whether a discipline or specialty is (III) more urban or rural in organization and (IV) more convergent or divergent. The urban–rural distinction refers to the question of how many people work on the same scientific problem. While in some areas of physics, for example, many people worldwide work on the same problem, it is easier for some humanities scholars and social scientists to look for an area in which there is little competition. The former would therefore be more urban, the latter more rural. Finally, the convergent–divergent distinction refers to whether the disciplinary identity and collective feeling are strong or whether there are tendencies toward division or fragmentation.

> Disciplinary communities that are convergent and tightly knit in terms of their fundamental ideologies, their common values, their share judgments of quality, their awareness of belonging to a unique tradition and the level of their agreement about what counts as appropriate disciplinary content and how it should be organized [...] are likely to occupy intellectual territories with well-defined external boundaries. (Becher and Trowler 2001, 59)

In contrast, disciplines where members lack a clear sense of belonging are often unable to defend their territories against usurpation by neighboring disciplines.

While the academic tribe continues to enjoy some popularity as a metaphor, this is less true of Becher's attempt to formulate them as analytical categories. Critics, including Becher's earlier co-author Paul Trowler (Trowler et al. 2012; Trowler 2014; Manathunga and Brew 2012), argued that the distinctions this conceptualization introduced (hard/soft, pure/applied, urban/rural, convergent/divergent) were in effect reproducing unjustified essentialisms. Yet, I have argued elsewhere that the metaphor of the academic tribes and their territories might be fruitfully developed in another way, one that follows the function and effect of academic "descent" and thus focuses on academic lineages (Dayé 2014). It is this semantic thrust that informs the theoretical framework presented in Chap. 4, where I will speak not of *academic*, but of *epistemic* tribes and territories.

Epistemic Culture

Compared to the other concepts discussed here, the concept of *epistemic culture* is of more recent origin. This may be due to the fact that the conceptual work on this concept has not yet been completed and that there are currently several approaches to using this term in the German-speaking world. An influential conceptualization of epistemic cultures is contained in the book of the same name by Karin Knorr Cetina. In it, she defines knowledge cultures as "amalgams of arrangements and mechanisms—bonded through affinity, necessity, and historical coincidence—which, in a given field, make up *how we know what we know*. Epistemic cultures are cultures that create and warrant knowledge" (Knorr Cetina 1999, 1; emphasis in original).

Epistemic cultures are therefore social arrangements in which knowledge claims are made and assessed.[3] Similar to the pairings of thought collective and thought style or academic tribe and territory, the concept of epistemic cultures has both a cognitive and a social component. In order

---

[3] In later works, Knorr Cetina's reflections on epistemic cultures as places where knowledge is generated and validated were complemented by a socialization dimension. For instance, Wolfgang Detel (2003, 2009) extended the concept of epistemic cultures by considering how scholars conveyed their background convictions and epistemic practices in educational institutions or student–teacher relationships though various channels of power.

to count as legitimate, knowledge claims have to be embedded in a web of practices, rituals, and methodological procedures, all of which are related to a set of norms and values. Epistemic cultures offer a reservoir of accepted practices, principles, and mechanisms that can be used to transform ideas and assertions into knowledge. Apart from other differences, it is the sustained focus on social practices that distinguishes the concept of epistemic culture from the Fleck's thought collective.

ACTOR-BASED COMMUNICATION NETWORKS

A second group of conceptualizations focuses not on the relations between social form and knowledge, but rather on describing fields of knowledge based on their internal information flows. Both the concept of the *scientific community* and the concept of the *invisible college* explore how (scientific) actors are located in communication networks.

The Scientific Community

Questions about the size, structure, and communication processes within scientific collectives come to the fore with another concept that can look back on a long and eventful history: that of the scientific community. Initially still a conceptually relatively open, everyday-language collective term for the entirety of those engaged in science, in the 1960s and 1970s, it was increasingly linked to the claim that the sociology of science should concern itself with studying scientists with the theoretical and methodological instruments prevailing in coeval social science. The theoretical enrichment of the concept of the scientific community is therefore possibly related to the Anglo-American tradition of community studies: social science studies in which social life in (small) communities was researched. The classics of this genre include Robert and Helen Lynd's studies in "Middletown," actually Muncie, Indiana (Lynd and Lynd 1929, 1937) or the research carried out under the aegis of W. Lloyd Warner in "Yankee City," actually Newburyport, Massachusetts (in particular Warner and Lunt 1941, 1942). This work looked at how status is distributed within communities and how moral order is established and controlled.

Similar questions are also explored in those works in which the scientific community is conceptualized in a theoretically richer way. The research focus is on the social structural characteristics of the scientific community, the applicable systems of reward and punishment, or, more generally, the institutions of social control and the normative substructure underlying the organization of scientific life. The communication and information channels within the collectives, their rituals, or the prevailing forms of goods production are researched to a greater extent than in Fleck's concept of the thought collective, for example.

However, Fleck's ideas on the connection between thought collectives and thought styles remained important. As already mentioned, they led the American historian of science Thomas S. Kuhn to the view that a sociology of the scientific community could provide information about the historical development of scientific knowledge. According to him, a scientific community consists of "the practitioners of a scientific specialty" who have undergone largely "similar educations and professional initiations" through which they "have absorbed the same technical literature and drawn many of the same lessons from it" (Kuhn 1970, 177). They have been socialized in a paradigm which informs their thinking and scientific doings. Like Fleck, Kuhn also sees the scientific community (Fleck's thought collective) as the bearer of a paradigm (Fleck's thought style); in contrast to Fleck, however, he also sees it as the basis on which the development of science can be explained in its basic features.

In contrast to the thought collective, the concept of the scientific community therefore focuses on the normative foundations of scientific activity (cf. Arnold 2020). It decides who receives awards for their work, how to deal with falsification and plagiarism, in short: it develops a normative structure including positive and negative sanctions, the most important channel of which is the recognition or denial of credibility (Merton 1968). However, this normative structure is not limited to the level of social interactions within the community. The scientific community is also an important instance of social control with regard to the continuation or development of the paradigm. "Colleagues influence decisions to select problems and techniques, to publish results, and to accept theories" (Hagstrom 1965, 1).

The concept of scientific community does not prejudge whether the normative structure is analyzed at the level of science in general or in smaller entities, such as disciplines or research fields. Arguments and good examples can be found for all the cases mentioned, although the latter do not usually come from the social sciences—Warren O. Hagstrom (1965) worked on physicists, and Daniel Kevles (1978) did the same from a historical perspective. An application of the concept of the scientific community in the history of sociology can build on these and other works, but must face two problems. Firstly, an analysis of sociology will have to do without a number of elements of Thomas Kuhn's theory, which is only rudimentarily presented here. Kuhn himself was of the opinion that sociology and other social sciences and humanities were multi-paradigmatic, which is why no paradigm shifts in the form of scientific revolutions took place in them (more on this in the section on scientific schools). The points of reference would then be less Kuhn's work than that of other sociologists of science active at the same time, such as the aforementioned Robert K. Merton and Warren O. Hagstrom, as well as the authors Diana Crane and Derek de Solla Price presented in the next section.

These authors, in turn—and this is the second problem—, have been repeatedly criticized for the fact that their theoretical approach gives priority to norm-compliant action in science and treats other action a priori as deviant. Inspired and partly supported by the larger debate between structural-functionalist and conflict-theoretical approaches, the concept of the scientific community is criticized for normatively disregarding internal conflicts, power struggles, norm breaches etc., in favor of an image of science dominated by unity and moral commitment. The extent to which this criticism is true is beyond the scope of this chapter.[4]

The Invisible College

Despite this criticism, the concept of the scientific community was a fruitful starting point in the 1960s and 1970s for attempts to describe this social form, its channels of information exchange, and its (normative) strucutres using methods of empirical social research (e.g., Price 1974). In the process, the US sociologist Diana Crane came across a phenomenon that she named the "invisible college," a term that, just like the scientific community, had also been used before. In line with other studies on scientific networks and citation frequencies, Crane (1972, esp. 49–56) found that within scientific fields or sub-disciplines, it is usually possible to identify local groups of scientists who cooperate with each other and are more likely to cite each other's work than those of researchers outside their

---

[4] Part of this accusation certainly arose from the attempts of subsequent researchers to differentiate themselves, who wanted to prove the innovative character of their perspective by denouncing the existing one as blind and one-sided. This is the only way to explain why concepts such as Merton's (1977, 1995) *microenvironments*—local social interdependencies from which ideas emerge—were and still are neglected in favor of a one-sided critique of his alleged "functionalist" bending (cf. Camic 2010).

vicinity. An exchange of information with other groups takes place, but tends to be limited to those group members who are the most productive in terms of research publications, and in the majority of cases these are the group leaders. On the one hand, they have more prestige within their own group and are often even its intellectual leaders; on the other hand, they also have relationships with other leaders or eminent subject representatives, exchange information with them, and pass on the information they receive to the other group members as required and as they see fit.

In contrast to the other concepts discussed so far, the invisible college is a concept derived from empirical observation. It is therefore historically closely linked to the use of methods of network analysis, citation analysis, and similar bibliometric techniques, although this does not mean that other methodological approaches are excluded in principle. However, the concept of the invisible college in the form developed by Crane and others is based on the measurement of communication relationships within scientific communities and approaches these with an interest in hierarchy and power relationships within researchers/groups.[5]

Group Structures and Group Dynamics

Some scholars of knowledge collectives have held a more sustained interest in exploring the socio-psychological dynamics at play in such communities, and have often taken inspiration from the research on small groups. Thus, they have addressed the emergence of different social roles within a group, or have explored how dynamics within such groups might trigger or suppress individual creativity.

The Scientific School

Around the time when the concepts of scientific community and invisible college were booming, another concept was also developed, namely, that of the scientific school (cf. Dayé 2015). A fundamental differentiation in

---

[5] Nicholas C. Mullins (1973) followed a similar theoretical interests to identify social structures based on communication and citation relationships. However, he developed his own concept of *theory groups*, which combines the research on citation patterns with an interest in school-like social forms of transmitting ideas, world views, and roles. Theory groups are a useful concept to analyze so-called multi-paradigmatic disciplines, like sociology: disciplines that are not centered around a single and shared set of basic principles (a paradigm), but where scholars work in parallel based on several sets of principles.

research on scientific schools is the one between a fairly general understanding of scientific schools as schools of thought, such as those that are sometimes presented in social science textbooks—structuralism, functionalism, institutionalism, symbolic interactionism, etc.—and a sociological concept of scientific schools as locally institutionalized knowledge collectives. The former has hardly been theorized and has many similarities with Kuhn's paradigm concept, which is why the following remarks are limited to the latter.

An institutionalized scientific school consists of a group of people who are working at the same place or have received scientific training there. Edward A. Tiryakian, who authored the probably best-known work on the sociological concept of the scientific school (Tiryakian 1979), built on the contemporary literature on the institutionalization of scientific disciplines and special fields (Ben-David and Collins 1966; Shils 1970; Clark 1972). However, in contrast to these works, he also drew a number of parallels to the development of religious denominations.

In both social forms, we can find a basic role differentiation between a founder-leader and their followers. Further, in both cases, the founder provides a world view, a "set of ideas, techniques and normative dispositions" (Tiryakian 1979, 217), which simultaneously separates the group from others and integrates its members. The members are endowed with an "intellectual sense of mission" (Tiryakian 1979, 217); they feel called upon to make the ideas of their master heard outside the local group. "The school may have a tacit sense of bringing salvation to the profession, that is, rescuing it from a state of stagnation and/or degradation" (Tiryakian 1979, 217).

In addition to this basic differentiation between founder-leader and followers, other positions often crystallize in scientific schools. Because founder-leaders, due to the novelty and unfamiliarity of their ideas, often lack the required intellectual distance to express their ideas in clear and accessible ways, schools often include an *interpreter*, "a person who knows the paradigm as an insider but who can translate it to outsiders so that they can see the relevance of the message" (Tiryakian 1979, 219). Often the interpreter also takes on the function of the *pragmatic organizer* who coordinates the infrastructure and the division of labor. However, these roles can also be filled by separate individuals.

There is also a group of *converts*, that is, people who are around the same age as the founder and have turned to the founder's world view after initial socialization in other worlds of thought. However, the younger *students* are more important because they are influenced by the ideas of the leader in a biographically decisive phase and have more energy (and lifetime) available to spread the paradigm. As "trusted lieutenants" (Tiryakian 1979, 219), they are also responsible for continuing the school after the leader has passed away, thus becoming the effective agents of the school's institutionalization.

Many scientific schools also have an *auxiliary*, a loyal foot soldier who helps in promoting the school and in seeking financial and organizational support, but who makes few, if any, intellectual contributions (Tiryakian 1979, 220). The latter also applies to the *patron*, who does not need to have a suitable professional background and only participates peripherally in the intellectual development of the school, but supports it through the use of social and/or economic capital.

Tiryakian developed his conceptualization as a critical continuation of Thomas Kuhn's (1970) reflections on the role of scientific revolutions in the development of scientific knowledge. Kuhn had argued that in the history of science and disciplines, phases of normal science could be distinguished from phases of revolutionary breaks. In phases of normal science, all representatives of a discipline align themselves with a more or less contradiction-free paradigm and use it almost like a recipe to solve scientific problems. In the reception of Kuhn's considerations, it has now been repeatedly argued that certain scientific fields, particularly in the humanities and cultural sciences, have never (or have not for a very long time) gone through phases of normal science. Rather, several paradigms coexist in them. The development of these fields cannot be explained by an alternation between epistemological harmony in phases of normal science and feverish innovation in phases of revolutionary disruption. Rather, the intellectual development of these fields results from the constant competition between different paradigms.

This is where Tiryakian comes in. He argues that the development of some scientific fields or disciplines, sociology among them, can be better understood with the concept of schools than with Kuhn's concept of paradigm. To make his point, Tiryakian explores how the different functions and roles within schools interact to create factors of academic success or failure. "A truly successful school," he writes, "is one which continues to recruit new members to its original founder and/or his lieutenants, and which continues to produce works of scientific eminence, for more than two or three generations" (Tiryakian 1979, 220). The assumption is that an academic generation comprises between five and ten cohorts of students.

Beyond their continued existence, other indicators of success can be identified. A school is successful when its publications are eagerly awaited and, upon publication, widely received by their peers; when its members are part of the discipline's important committees and jurisdictional bodies; and when they are appointed to prestigious positions. Furthermore, it seems to help a school in the battle for attention if it is institutionally linked to a university with a high reputation and if it is located in a larger city. "This makes it easier for the leader to have access to communication channels which inform him [!] of the advanced state of the art in other disciplines, to communicate with colleagues in other disciplines, and to attract highly gifted students who have to pay some attention to later employment opportunities" (Tiryakian 1979, 223).

Two further success factors concern the publication market. First, the school would do well to publish its own journal or book series. On the one hand, this helps to ensure that the intellectual products and research results from the members of the school can be communicated to the larger audience of the disciplines; on the other hand, a journal of its own can also foster the capacity of the school to keep students within its orbit who, after having completed their training, move on to places emotionally and intellectually distant to the school. Second, it is also important for the identity of a school and thus for its cohesion that there is a kind of manifesto, a document that summarizes the mission and paradigm of the school, as this can be used to train students in other places than the school or even after the death of the school's founding generation.

Collaborative Circles

Tiryakian's conceptualization of scientific schools conceived of a school as an institutionalized social form in which certain tasks—research, teaching, publication, public presence—must be jointly organized and completed. A more recent concept that does not presuppose such institutionalization is the concept of collaborative circles introduced by Michael P. Farrell (2001). Informed by social-psychological research on creativity, Farrell defines a collaborative circle as "a primary group consisting of peers who share similar occupational goals and who, through long periods of dialogue and collaboration, negotiate a common vision that guides their work. The vision consists of a shared set of assumptions about their discipline, including what constitutes good work, how to work, what subjects are worth working on, and how to think about them" (Farrell 2001, 11).

Collaborative circles combine the dynamics of groups of friends and work groups. As Farrell shows with reference to various artist groups—among them the Inklings around C. S. Lewis and J. R. R. Tolkien and the French Impressionists—, the development of a collaborative circle follows a pattern that can be divided into seven phases (cf. in particular Farrell 2001, pp. 17–26). (*1*) *Formation*: a more or less stable group of like-minded people with similar interests is formed. However, these interests initially remain diffuse; the focus is on friendships. (*2*) *Rebellion against authority*: against the background of mutual trust arising from friendships, group members discover a shared antipathy toward authority in a particular field. This shared antipathy is communicatively reinforced and thus strengthens group cohesion. (*3*) *Negotiating a new vision*: the emotional energy generated by the shared antipathy is channeled into the search for a group goal, a new vision to replace that of the old authorities. (*4*) *The creative work stage*: this is followed by a phase of high productivity among the group members, both individually and in groups. The principles set out in the vision are realized in works that are first and foremost presented to the other group members. (*5*) *The collective action stage*: the group members decide on joint projects, such as the organization of an exhibition or the founding of a magazine. In this phase, the degree of division of labor and consequently of internal group organization increases, which is why hierarchical differences between the members become entrenched here at the latest. (*6*) *The separation stage*: often due to the efforts of collective action, the group slowly begins to disintegrate. Conflicts accumulate and undermine cohesion. In creative professions, the individuality of the creative person is an important part of their professional ethos, which reinforces the centrifugal process. (*7*) *The nostalgic reunion stage*: years or decades after the circle has split up, its members meet again and look for things in common and things that divide them.

Science–Policy Nexus

One similarity of all the conceptualizations discussed above was the unquestioned boundary between science and policy. This demarcation, it was argued, was not a given, but was created in painstaking detail by interested actors pursuing a wide variety of social strategies (cf. Gieryn 1999). The fourth type of conceptualizations discussed in this chapter has critically taken aim at this differentiation. They argued that if a functional differentiation ever existed between these two social systems, the twentieth century had aptly shown the importance of spheres where science and policy overlapped. From the various uses of science for political means during the Cold War—think of the hydrogen bomb, the space race, or the role of science diplomacy (Moore 2008)—to the addition of risk management tasks to the responsibilities of states (Rothstein et al. 2006) and the emergence of regulatory science (Jasanoff 1990), the relevance of the science–policy nexus cannot be overstated, in terms of both political and intellectual impact. *Epistemic community* and *scientific/intellectual movement* are two conceptualizations to explore this nexus.

Epistemic Community

Proposed by the political scientist Peter M. Haas (1992a, 1992b), *epistemic communities* are networks of people who are competent and recognized as experts on a specific topic. Although these people may have different professional backgrounds and do not necessarily have to have a scientific-academic education, they have the following things in common (cf. Haas 1992a, 3): (*1*) they share a set of normative and principled beliefs that supports the collective and coordinated actions of the members of the community. (*2*) Based on their shared knowledge and interpretations of the world, they fundamentally agree on the causal relationships governing their field of knowledge, and from this, they derive political options for action. (*3*) They have a shared understanding of the criteria that determine whether a knowledge claim can be described as valid or not. And (*4*) they participate in a common policy enterprise—in other words, they actively try to apply their knowledge to one (or more) defined problem(s) and, "presumably out of the conviction that human welfare will be enhanced as a consequence" (Haas 1992a, 3), pave the way for their knowledge's impact on society.

Scientific/Intellectual Movements (SIMs)

American sociologists Scott Frickel and Neil Gross (2005) introduced the term scientific/intellectual movements (SIMs) to capture the empirical phenomenon that theoretical traditions or sometimes even scientific specialties may in their early stages look very much like social movements. People join in an organized, collective effort to help establish, and at best institutionalize, a particular idea or a coherent set of ideas. These ideas are perceived as having the power to transform the dominant ways of thinking and thus promise innovation, sometimes even in terms of advancing a public good. The transformation that SIMs wish to achieve are not gradual; rather, they "involve dramatic breaks with past practices" (Frickel and Gross 2005, 207). Due to their transformative potential, these new ideas are always contentious—moreover, they are inherently political: "every program for intellectual change involves a desire to alter the configuration of social positions within or across intellectual fields in which power, attention, and other scarce resources are unequally distributed," Frickel and Gross (2005, 207) argue with reference to Pierre Bourdieu. However, they add that not every individual must be motivated by strategic careerism, as sometimes suggested. Scholars may simply believe strongly in the moral, intellectual, or social value of the transformations that the SIM achieves to implement.

SIMs are transitionary figures: they either solidify into disciplines or other social formations, or they disappear when the initial energy gets lost on the resistance—or the inertia—of the established system. A decisive factor in the fate of a SIM is whether the movement participants, in particular those who are most visible, are able to frame the movement's ideas "in ways that resonate with the concerns of those who inhabit an intellectual field or fields" (Frickel and Gross 2005, 221).

Conclusion

This chapter introduced a series of sociological conceptualizations of collectives and groups in the sciences and humanities. It discussed them according to their respective analytical focus. Some conceptualizations emphasize the relations between social form/practices and knowledge and attempt to identify the dynamics that govern these relations. Others focus on the actor-based communication networks without which science would not exist. Still other concepts take aim at the structures of and internal dynamics within groups of scientists or scholars. And a final fourth category of concepts focus on the science–policy nexus and explain how knowledge creation is informed by an interested and action-oriented demand for knowledge.

However, futures studies and the sociology of the future do not neatly fall into one of these concepts. Admittedly, futures studies shows characteristics of an epistemic community: the community comprises not only knowledge-oriented scholars but also action-oriented decision-makers; and indeed, the strength of the field is sometimes found in exactly its ability to bridge between different parts of society. But at the same time, epistemic communities embark on a common policy enterprise—which is not the case with futures studies.

The sociology of the future, on the other hand, is a part of an academic discipline. By discipline, we usually understand the parallelism of a demarcated branch of knowledge, its organization in terms of research environments (professorships and university departments, journals, publishers, funding agencies), and its means of social reproduction (programs of academic training) (Shils 1970; Jacobs 2014). But as a field of interest within sociology, the sociology of the future also lacks institutional autonomy: there are no dedicated journals, only few professorships, no textbooks, and almost no sections within the relevant scholarly associations.

In short, which of these conceptualizations match the actual shape of futures studies and the sociology of the future remains an empirical question. This is the objective of the studies presented in this book. The overview provided in this chapter paves the way for better understanding the capacities and limitations of the theoretical frame and the related research design, which are introduced in the next chapter.

References

Arnold, Markus. 2020. Scientific Communities. A History of Theories and Concepts. In *Franz Brentano and Austrian Philosophy*, Vienna Circle Institute Yearbook, ed. D. Fisette, G. Fréchette, and F. Stadler, 387–424. Cham: Springer.

Becher, Tony. 1989. *Academic Tribes and Territories: Intellectual Enquiry and the Cultures of Disciplines.* Milton Keynes (UK), Bristol (PA): Open University Press.

Becher, Tony, and Paul Trowler. 2001. *Academic Tribes and Territories: Intellectual Enquiry and the Culture of Disciplines.* 2nd ed. Buckingham, Philadelphia (PA): Open University Press.

Ben-David, Joseph, and Randall Collins. 1966. Social Factors in the Origins of a New Science: The Case of Psychology. *American Sociological Review* 31:451–465. https://doi.org/10.2307/2090769.

Bessner, Daniel. 2018. *Democracy in Exile: Hans Speier and the Rise of the Defense Intellectual.* In *The United States in the World.* Ithaca, NY: Cornell University Press.

Camic, Charles. 2010. How Merton Sociologizes the History of Ideas. In *Robert K. Merton: Sociology of Science and Sociology as Science*, ed. Craig Calhoun, 273–295. New York: Columbia University Press.

Clark, Terry N. 1972. The Stages of Scientific Institutionalization. *International Social Science Journal* 24:658–670.

Crane, Diana. 1972. *Invisible Colleges: Diffusion of Knowledge in Scientific Communities*. Chicago, London: The University of Chicago Press.
Dayé, Christian. 2014. In fremden Territorien: Delphi, Political Gaming und die subkutane Bedeutung tribaler Wissenskulturen. *Österreichische Zeitschrift für Geschichtswissenschaften* 25:83–115.
Dayé, Christian. 2015. Schools in the Social and Behavioral Sciences: Concepts and Historical Relevance. In *International Encyclopedia of the Social and Behavioral Sciences*, ed. James D. Wright, vol. 21, 2nd ed., 128–133. Elsevier.
Dayé, Christian. 2018. How to Train Your Oracle: The Delphi Method and Its Turbulent Youth in Operations Research and the Policy Sciences. *Social Studies of Science* 48:846–868. https://doi.org/10.1177/0306312718798497.
Detel, Wolfgang. 2003. Wissenskulturen und epistemische Praktiken. In *Wissenskulturen: Beiträge zu einem forschungsstrategischen Konzept*, ed. Johannes Fried and Thomas Kailer, 119–132. Berlin: Akademie Verlag.
Detel, Wolfgang. 2009. Wissenskulturen und universelle Rationalität. In *Wissenskulturen: über die Erzeugung und Weitergabe von Wissen*, ed. Johannes Fried and Michael Stolleis, 181–214. Campus Verlag.
Egloff, Rainer. 2011. Evolution des Erkennens. In *Schlüsselwerke des Konstruktivismus*, ed. Bernhard Pörksen, 60–77. VS Verlag für Sozialwissenschaften. https://doi.org/10.1007/978-3-531-93069-5_4.
Farrell, Michael P. 2001. *Collaborative Circles: Friendship Dynamics & Creative Work*. Chicago, London: The University of Chicago Press.
Fleck, Ludwik. 1979. *Genesis and Development of a Scientific Fact*. Chicago: University of Chicago Press.
Foucault, Michel. 2002. *The Order of Things: An Archaeology of the Human Sciences. Routledge Classics*. London, New York: Routledge.
Frickel, Scott, and Neil Gross. 2005. A General Theory of Scientific/Intellectual Movements. *American Sociological Review* 70:204–232. https://doi.org/10.1177/000312240507000202.
Fried, Morton H. 1966. On the Concepts of "Tribe" and "Tribal Society". *Transactions of the New York Academy of Sciences* 28:527–540.
Fried, Morton H. 1975. *The Notion of Tribe*. Menlo Park (CA), Reading (MA), London, Amsterdam, Don Mills (ON), Sydney: Cummings Pub. Co.
Gieryn, Thomas F. 1999. *Cultural Boundaries of Science: Credibility on the Line*. Chicago, London: The University of Chicago Press.
Haas, Peter M. 1992a. Introduction: Epistemic Communities and International Policy Coordination. *International Organization* 46:1–35.
Haas, Peter M. 1992b. Banning Chlorofluorocarbons: Epistemic Community Efforts to Protect Stratospheric Ozone. *International Organization* 46:187–224.
Hagstrom, Warren O. 1965. *The Scientific Community*. Carbondale, Edwardsville: Southern Illinois University Press.

Jacobs, Jerry A. 2014. *In Defense of Disciplines: Interdisciplinarity and Specialization in the Research University.* Chicago, London: The University of Chicago Press.
Jasanoff, Sheila. 1990. *The Fifth Branch. Science Advisers as Policymakers.* Cambridge (MA), London: Harvard University Press.
Kevles, Daniel J. 1978. *The Physicists: The History of a Scientific Community in Modern America.* New York: Knopf.
Knorr Cetina, Karin. 1999. *Epistemic Cultures. How the Sciences Make Knowledge.* Cambridge (MA): Harvard University Press.
Kuhn, Thomas S. 1970. *The Structure of Scientific Revolutions.* 2nd ed. Enlarged. International Encyclopedia of Unified Science, Volume II, Number 2. Chicago: University of Chicago Press.
Lynd, Robert S., and Helen Merrell Lynd. 1929. *Middletown: A Study in Contemporary American Culture.* New York: Harcourt, Brace and Company.
Lynd, Robert S., and Helen Merrell Lynd. 1937. *Middletown in Transition: A Study in Cultural Conflicts.* New York: Harcourt, Brace and Company.
Manathunga, Catherine, and Angela Brew. 2012. Beyond Tribes and Territories: New Metaphors for New Times. In *Tribes and Territories in the 21st-Century: Rethinking the Significance of Disciplines in Higher Education,* ed. Paul Trowler, Murray Saunders, and Veronica Bamber, 44–56. London; New York: Routledge.
Merton, Robert K. 1968. The Matthew Effect in Science. *Science* 159:56–63.
Merton, Robert K. 1977. The Sociology of Science: An Episodic Memoir. In *The Sociology of Science in Europe,* ed. Robert K. Merton and Jerry Gaston, 3–141. Carbondale, Ill: Southern Illinois University Press.
Merton, Robert K. 1995. Opportunity Structure: The Emergence, Diffusion, and Differentiation of a Sociological Concept, 1930s–1950s. In *The legacy of anomie theory,* ed. Freda Adler and William S. Laufer, 3–78. New Brunswick, N.J.: Transaction Publishers.
Moore, Kelly. 2008. *Disrupting Science. Social Movements, American Scientists, and the Politics of the Military, 1945–1975.* Princeton and Oxford: Princeton University Press.
Mullins, Nicholas C. 1973. *Theories and Theory Groups in Contemporary American Sociology.* New York: Harper & Row.
Price, Derek J. Solla. 1974. *Little Science, Big Science. Von der Studierstube zur Großforschung.* Frankfurt am Main: Suhrkamp.
Rothstein, Henry, Michael Huber, and George Gaskell. 2006. A Theory of Risk Colonization: The Spiralling Regulatory Logics of Societal and Institutional Risk. *Economy and Society* 35:91–112.
Seefried, Elke. 2014. Steering the Future. The Emergence of "Western" Futures Research and Its Production of Expertise, 1950s to early 1970s. *European Journal of Futures Research* 2: Article 29, 12 pages. https://doi.org/10.1007/s40309-013-0029-y.

Seefried, Elke. 2015a. Die Gestaltbarkeit der Zukunft und ihre Grenzen. Zur Entstehung der Zukunftsforschung. *Zeitschrift für Zukunftsforschung* 4:5–31.

Seefried, Elke. 2015b. *Zukünfte. Aufstieg und Krise der Zukunftsforschung 1945–1980.* Berlin: Walter de Gruyter.

Shils, Edward. 1970. Tradition, Ecology, and Institution in the History of Sociology. *Daedalus* 99:760–825.

Tiryakian, Edward A. 1979. The Significance of Schools in the Development of Sociology. In *Contemporary Issues in Theory and Research. A Metasociological Perspective*, ed. William E. Snizek, Ellsworth R. Fuhrman, and Michael K. Miller, 211–233. London: Aldwych Press.

Tolon, Kaya. 2012. Future Studies: A New Social Science Rooted in Cold War Strategic Thinking. In *Cold War Social Science: Knowledge Production, Liberal Democracy, and Human Nature*, ed. Mark Solovey and Hamilton Cravens, 45–62. New York: Palgrave Macmillan.

Trowler, Paul. 2014. Academic Tribes and Territories: The Theoretical Trajectory. *Österreichische Zeitschrift für Geschichtswissenschaften* 25:17–26.

Trowler, Paul, Murray Saunders, and Veronica Bamber, eds. 2012. *Tribes and Territories in the 21st-Century: Rethinking the Significance of Disciplines in Higher Education*. London; New York: Routledge.

Warner, W. Lloyd, and Paul S. Lunt. 1941. *The Social Life of a Modern Community*. New Haven; London: Yale University Press; H. Milford, Oxford University Press.

Warner, W. Lloyd, and Paul S. Lunt. 1942. *The Status System of a Modern Community*. New Haven; London: Yale University Press; H. Milford, Oxford University Press.

CHAPTER 4

Researching Scientific Attention Spaces: Epistemic Tribes and Territories

Abstract This chapter introduces the theoretical framework and the research design of the scientometric studies of futures studies and the sociology of the future. The central concept of the theoretical framework is the knowledge collective, which over given periods of time entertains different attention spaces. Two options to map such attention spaces are discussed: first, researchers can focus on which references are used to support the claims made in publications. As this concerns the tracing of lineages of ideas, the term epistemic tribe is proposed to address the clusters found in this attention space. Second, researchers can focus on the topics that are predominantly discussed within an attention space. This dimension is explored as the territories claimed by the members of the knowledge collective under scrutiny. In concluding, the chapter describes the data retrieval procedures used and justifies the use of Elsevier's Scopus database.

Keywords Co-citation analysis • Co-occurrence analysis • Bibliometric data • Scientometrics • Sociology of science

INTRODUCTION

This chapter introduces the theoretical framework for the scientometric studies of the two fields of scientific futures thinking that are presented in Chaps. 5 and 6. In short, this framework focuses on the notion of

© The Author(s), under exclusive license to Springer Nature Switzerland AG 2025
C. Dayé, *Futures Thinking*,
https://doi.org/10.1007/978-3-031-91941-1_4

attention space and analyzes relations between ideas and topics within this attention space. In other words, it describes what themes are dominating a given attention space, and which sources the contributions defining this attention space reference to support their claims. For reasons that are explained below, I suggest the terms *epistemic tribes and territories* to capture this double interest.

Based on this theoretical framework, the chapter proceeds to present the research design and the data retrieval procedures. Data come from a bibliometric database of scientific literature. To analyze them, two procedures were used that are well established in scientometrics, that is, the quantitative study of science: co-citation analysis and co-occurrence analysis. While co-citation analysis allows to explore lineages of ideas and arguments, and thus is used to analyze *epistemic tribes*, co-occurrence analysis allows to identify the most important topics within an intellectual attention space—in other words, the *territories* claimed by the epistemic tribes.

Theorizing the Attention Space: Epistemic Tribes and Territories

The theoretical framework developed below combines and slightly reconfigures elements and ideas that appear in existing conceptualizations (as introduced in Chap. 3). It is thus not new, in the sense of formulating ideas that have not yet been put forth, but innovative, in the Schumpeterian sense that it combines existing elements in a new way.

The central notion of this framework is the *attention space*. This is a term already used by some authors, most prominently perhaps by Randall Collins, who in his seminal book *The Sociology of Philosophies* (Collins 1998) described the development of philosophy as a continued struggle over the intellectual attention space. In a similar fashion, German scholar and architect Georg Franck has used the term attention space in the 1990s to analyze recent cultural phenomena as part of a transformation toward an economy of attention (Franck 1998, 2019).

In the framework used in this book, the spatial dimension of the attention space is emphasized. The attention space of a knowledge collective comprises the topics and issues that the knowledge collective discusses and publishes on in a defined period of time.

Attention spaces show various structural characteristics, two of which are explored in this book. First, we identify the important points of reference for the arguments put forth in the attention space. As this interest is concerned with tracing lineages of theoretical (or methodological) argumentation, I introduce the concept of *epistemic tribe* to describe the web of descent that publications create through citing earlier works. This focus on lineage is in line with an earlier study of mine (Dayé 2014), but at the same time a crucial difference to how Becher and Trowler made use of the metaphor of a tribe (Becher 1989; Becher and Trowler 2001; Trowler et al. 2012). Further, using the adjective epistemic instead of academic emphasizes that we are not in the cultural space of academia—no university, no administration, no students, no conferences, no grants—, but in the more abstract space of ideas that are put forth in scientific publications. Members of an epistemic tribe tend to invoke the same sources in support of their ideas and arguments.

Critical observers may contest this last statement by pointing out that it is quite common to also cite sources just in order to refute them, that is, to distance oneself from the ideas put forth in the source. This is correct. However, such negative citations can still be taken to be an indicator of acknowledging the source as a legitimate member of the same tribe whose voice had to be respected even if one disagreed (Catalini et al. 2015; Xu et al. 2022).

Second, attention spaces can also be investigated in terms of the content they cover—that is, the *territories* that the knowledge collective inhabits over a particular period or at a particular point in time. Research topics have careers; they emerge and begin to blossom, and while some may see a steep increase in interest and publication output followed by a similarly quick disappearance (and occasionally, re-discovery), others may stay around for longer periods without ever being hyped.

This framework is admittedly, and intentionally, lean in terms of theory. It does not propose a radically new way of seeing science, or of conceiving of the relation between scientific collectives and ideas. Its advantage is that it is closely aligned to the empirical materials with which it deals and thus makes sure that its claims are supported. This also matches with the exploratory thrust of the two scientometric methods.

There exist a few studies that approach futures studies through bibliometric data and scientometric network analyses. In an attempt to describe the historical trajectories of research themes and their diffusion across publications, Lu et al. (2016) subjected Web of Science (WoS) data to a main path analysis. Further, Fergnani (2019) used bibliometric data to identify clusters of themes in contemporary publications.

As regards the sociology of the future, Jens Beckert and Lisa Suckert (2021) carried out a comprehensive study where they combined both quantitative and qualitative steps of analysis to explore the attention space described by their data. The study, however, focuses on one particular type of sociological interest in the future, that is, how sociologists have empirically studied actors' perceptions of the future. This focus allows them to describe in richer detail the development of this particular research agenda; yet, the research design proposed below, while not offering the same degree of detailedness, comprises, in principle, all strands of sociological research on the future.[1]

Compared to these studies, the theoretical frame used here—and the research design that operationalizes it—enable us to go one step further. The focus of the research just mentioned is on identifying clusters and thus on differences between areas within a scientific field. In contrast, the research design applied in this book offers a perspective that combines both differences and similarities. On the one hand, co-citation and co-occurrence analyses indeed deliver a list of clusters, thus focusing on structural differences within the attention space; on the other hand, however, these differences are always interpreted in relation to the overall network, and the relations between the clusters are also systematically considered. Due to this combination of perspectives, the relatedness and occasionally even closeness of elements of different clusters also comes into view. This is important as it helps to counter-balance the concentration on fragmentation within an intellectual attention space that sometimes dominates the reflective discourses within the sciences.

THE RESEARCH DESIGN

Due to both its leanness and the closeness to the capacities of the envisaged methods of analysis, the operationalization of the theoretical framework is straightforward. Three concepts have to be operationalized: the knowledge community and two options to explore structures of its intellectual attention space: epistemic tribes and territories.

The knowledge community is operationalized through the search terms used in retrieving data from the scientific literature database. These have

---

[1] Another problem of Beckert and Suckert's (2021) study is their reliance on the Web of Science (WoS) database. As explained below, WoS has certain important shortcomings that Clarivate's Scopus can level out, at least to a certain degree.

to be selected diligently to ensure that the claims and interpretations resulting from the analysis truly concern the envisaged knowledge community. As indicated above, the knowledge collectives of interest in the studies presented in Chaps. 5 and 6 are futures studies and the sociology of the future.

The knowledge collective maintains an intellectual attention space, which is dynamic and can be explored for various characteristics. This attention space is operationally defined by the mappings that result from the scientometric procedures. Co-citation analysis and co-occurrence analysis both map their networks into a low-dimensional, non-Euclidean space (usually, they use two dimensions). Thus, the notion of attention space used in this book is the space that results from these methods.

Two different types of attention spaces are analyzed in this book: one that concerns the sources which are cited to clarify the arguments made—thus building networks of tribal lineage—, and the topics explored—thus, the territories covered by the knowledge community. The size and shape of epistemic tribes within an attention space as well as their interrelations are analyzed by co-citation analysis, while territories are explored through co-occurrence analysis.

Both co-citation analysis and co-occurrence analysis are established techniques in scientometrics (Marshakova 1973, 1981; Small 1973, 1980; Braam et al. 1991a, 1991b; Osareh 1996a, 1996b). They can be used for a variety of objectives. In recent years, however, they have seen increased use as an approach to exploring basic structures in information spaces, to use the general term for what is called attention space here (Tijssen and Van Raan 1994).

Co-citation builds on notions developed within (social) network analysis and creates a network based on the relations between pairs of references. In the terminology of network analysis, any two references that both appear in the list of references of an article form a *dyad*, with each being reference being a *node*, and the fact that they are cited in the same text is used to define the *edge*, that is, the line between the nodes.[2] Given that in scientometrics, one usually does not explore one text, but a larger corpus of numerous texts, the more frequent a dyad is found, the more pronounced the edge between the two nodes. The nodes are then mapped onto a low-dimensional Euclidean space, and objects that are often cited

---

[2] Useful introductions to social network analysis are Prell (2012), Borgatti et al. (2013), Scott (2017), and Yang et al. (2017).

together are closer to each other and marked with stronger edges. Based on this basic mechanism, a co-citation analysis also identifies clusters of references that are more frequently cited together. These clusters can then be interpreted as the structures of the attention space described by the search terms.

Co-occurrence analysis also relies on the network analytical procedures described above; yet, instead of cited sources, it takes words as nodes and explores how often they are mentioned in a given corpus (Harris 1957). In our case, these words are the keywords provided by the authors of the scientific publications upon submission. Just like with co-citation analysis, dyads of keywords, the most prominent keywords, are then used to create network visualizations. The frequency of how often a keyword dyad is found is used to determine the proximity of the two keywords as nodes in the network.

The software used for the analysis is VOSviewer, an open-source software developed by Nees Jan van Eck and Ludo Waltman at the Centre for Science and Technology Studies of Leiden University, the Netherlands.[3] This software provides an easy-to-use solution for analyzing bibliometric data. The clustering implemented in VOSviewer follows a procedure described in Waltman et al. (2010).

The Data

While quite a few studies rely on Clarivate's literature database Web of Science (WoS) for their analyses, after a few comparisons, it was decided that the analyses presented on these pages should use Elsevier's Scopus. The findings of the initial comparison phase corroborated various earlier studies, which have repeatedly shown Scopus to be more preferable to WoS. First, Scopus lists significantly more journals than WoS. According to calculations from 2016, around 35% of the social science journals listed in these databases appeared in both (overlap), while a further 63% appeared exclusively in Scopus and only 1% were listed in WoS but not in Scopus (cf. Mongeon and Paul-Hus 2016; see also Bauschmann and Ahnert 2017). This may also be the main reason why in the preparatory comparisons done for this book, the search query used to capture the attention space of the sociology of the future only yielded slightly more than half (n = 547) of the number of hits in WoS than in Scopus (n = 1039).

---

[3] See https://www.vosviewer.com/, last visited 11 February 2025.

In addition, the data provided by Scopus delivered more plausible results compared to WoS. Using the search commands described below, the WoS dataset was missing entries that should have been included based on the search command and that are also generally available in the database.[4] These implausibilities suggested that the WoS dataset should at most be used for cautious validation of the findings drawn from Scopus.

Thirdly, the reference section in Scopus is considerably better standardized compared to WoS. This is particularly important for the co-citation analysis. Although there were still aspects in the data sets that had to be corrected (see below for details), comparisons supported the impression that this required significantly less effort than cleaning the data extracted from WoS, where references sometimes even lacked the name(s) of the author(s) or even the title.

Fourthly, compared to WoS, Scopus covered a much broader time axis. For example, while the oldest publication in the WoS dataset for the sociology of the future was from 1956, the oldest publication in the Scopus dataset was published as early as 1917. In addition to this, Scopus returned fifteen further hits from the period before 1956.

Of course, such an approach has to contend with a number of shortcomings. On the one hand, this concerns the databases themselves, whose biases are well known: both platforms favor publications that are written in English, by Western authors, and belong to the natural and technical sciences (cf. Tennant 2020, 1; see also Mongeon and Paul-Hus 2016; Bauschmann and Ahnert 2017). Tennant's (2020, 2) judgment that the use of these services perpetuates a Western hegemony of the global scientific space is not so easy to dismiss. Clarivate, the company behind Web of Science, is based in London, while Elsevier is based in Amsterdam. Further inadequacies admittedly arise from the search queries: while a term like "sociolog*" covers languages such as Spanish, Dutch, Portuguese, and

---

[4] In the case of the sociology of the future, this particularly affected the publications of Markus Schulz, who, as a high-profile author, has several entries in the Scopus dataset but does not appear at all in the WoS dataset—even though the articles in question can be found in WoS and should have been included in the search. Take Schulz's (2011) essays "The values of global futures" in *Current Sociology*, "Future moves: Forward-oriented studies of culture, society, and technology" in *Current Sociology* (Schulz 2015), and "Debating futures: Global trends, alternative visions, and public discourse" in *International Sociology* (Schulz 2016). All three articles have "future" or "futures" in the title, were published in journals that have sociology in the title, and—as a targeted search shows—are generally listed in WoS. Yet, they were missing from the exported dataset.

French, large language communities like Arabic, Mandarin, Hindi, and German are excluded.

All these limitations make it clear that the approach presented here does not, of course, enable the surveying of a scientific field in the strict sense, but rather merely an exploration of patterns of recognition and attention within a hegemonically defined field of knowledge.

Futures Studies

In order to capture the knowledge collective of futures studies, the search prompt selected all entries where one (or several) of the terms {futures research}, {futures studies}, or {futurology} appeared in one or more of these categories: topic, title, abstract, keywords provided by the author, and keywords that were assigned by the database. The restriction to these fields was motivated by the wish to avoid the title of the journal being the only decisive factor in selection. This meant that the fact that an article was in, for example, the *Journal of Futures Studies* or the *European Journal of Futures Research* was per se not deemed sufficient for selection.

Carried out on 4 January 2025, this search returned 13,413 entries.

Several steps of data washing have been carried out with the data, all of them ensuring that the same references have a uniform entry. For instance, there existed various versions of references citing Wendell Bell's *Foundations of Futures Studies*, whose two volumes have seen several new editions.[5]

Sociology of the Future

For the sociology of the future, the data was retrieved with the following search query: Source Title = sociolog* AND Article Title = future OR futures. The first part of the query restricted the search to those journals that clearly communicated their disciplinary classification to the outside world by using the name of the discipline. Journals from Science and Technology Studies or other interdisciplinary fields were thus excluded. From the journals thus selected, the second part of the search query retrieved those articles whose titles contained the terms "future" or "futures."

---

[5] The corrections have been carefully documented and will be distributed upon request by the author, together with the data.

On 4 January 2025, this search query returned 1039 hits. Again, a series of data washing steps had to be taken, including unifying citations of Bell's Foundations of Futures Studies, Eleonora Masini's *Why Futures Studies?* (Masini 1993), or the various editions of Peter Schwartz' *The Art of the Long View* (e.g., Schwartz 1997).

Conclusion

This chapter introduced and justified the theoretical framework of the studies described in the subsequent chapter. Put briefly, knowledge collectives are conceived of dealing with restricted attention spaces, and these attention spaces can be assessed empirically through an analysis of the respective collective's publication output. Two ways to assess the attention spaces of collectives are foregrounded in this book: the interest in lineages of ideas and the dominance of certain topics. The terms epistemic tribes and territories were proposed as two types of (mapping and) assessing attention spaces.

The chapter then went on to show how this theoretical framework informed the research design and the operationalizations used in the study. When using databases of scientific literature, knowledge collectives can be operationalized through a diligent formulation of the search prompts. The prompts used as well as the number of entries retrieved from the Scopus database are given in Table 4.1.

The next chapter presents the results of the scientometric analyses for the knowledge collective of futures studies. As explained above, the research design uses co-citation analysis to explore epistemic tribes, and co-occurrence analysis to explore their territories.

Table 4.1 Data characteristics

Knowledge collective	Futures studies	Sociology of the future
Operationalization/ search prompt	Article title OR Abstract OR Keywords = "futures research" OR "futures studies" OR "futurology"	Source title = "sociology*" AND Article title = "future" OR "futures"
Literature database	Scopus	Scopus
Results	13,413 entries	1039 entries
Date of data retrieval	4 Jan 2025	21 Aug 2024

References

Bauschmann, Martin, and Carolin Ahnert. 2017. *Vergleich von Web of Science und Scopus im Hinblick auf den Informationsbedarf an der TU Chemnitz.* Erstveröffentlichung Mai 2016, teilaktualisierte Fassung vom Mai 2017. Chemnitz: TU Chemnitz.

Becher, Tony. 1989. *Academic Tribes and Territories: Intellectual Enquiry and the Cultures of Disciplines.* Milton Keynes (UK), Bristol (PA): Open University Press.

Becher, Tony, and Paul Trowler. 2001. *Academic Tribes and Territories: Intellectual Enquiry and the Culture of Disciplines.* 2nd ed. Buckingham, Philadelphia (PA): Open University Press.

Beckert, Jens, and Lisa Suckert. 2021. The Future as a Social Fact. The Analysis of Perceptions of the Future in Sociology. *Poetics* 84:101499. https://doi.org/10.1016/j.poetic.2020.101499.

Borgatti, Stephen P., Martin G. Everett, and Jeffrey C. Johnson. 2013. *Analyzing Social Networks.* Los Angeles, London, New Delhi, Singapore: SAGE.

Braam, Robert R., Henk F. Moed, and Anthony F. J. van Raan. 1991a. Mapping of Science by Combined Co-citation and Word Analysis. I. Structural Aspects. *Journal of the American Society for Information Science* 42:233–251. https://doi.org/10.1002/(SICI)1097-4571(199105)42:4<233::AID-ASI1>3.0.CO;2-I.

Braam, Robert R., Henk F. Moed, and Anthony F. J. van Raan. 1991b. Mapping of Science by Combined Co-citation and Word Analysis. II: Dynamical Aspects. *Journal of the American Society for Information Science* 42:252–266. https://doi.org/10.1002/(SICI)1097-4571(199105)42:4<252::AID-ASI2>3.0.CO;2-G.

Catalini, Christian, Nicola Lacetera, and Alexander Oettl. 2015. The Incidence and Role of Negative Citations in Science. *Proceedings of the National Academy of Sciences of the United States of America* 112:13823–13826. https://doi.org/10.1073/pnas.1502280112.

Collins, Randall. 1998. *The Sociology of Philosophies: A Global Theory of Intellectual Change.* Cambridge (MA), London: Harvard University Press.

Dayé, Christian. 2014. In fremden Territorien: Delphi, Political Gaming und die subkutane Bedeutung tribaler Wissenskulturen. *Österreichische Zeitschrift für Geschichtswissenschaften* 25:83–115.

Fergnani, Alessandro. 2019. Mapping Futures Studies Scholarship from 1968 to Present: A Bibliometric Review of Thematic Clusters, Research Trends, and Research Gaps. *Futures* 105:104–123. https://doi.org/10.1016/j.futures.2018.09.007.

Franck, Georg. 1998. *Ökonomie der Aufmerksamkeit.* München: Hanser.

Franck, Georg. 2019. The Economy of Attention. *Journal of Sociology* 55:8–19. https://doi.org/10.1177/1440783318811778.

Harris, Zellig S. 1957. Co-Occurrence and Transformation in Linguistic Structure. Language 33. *Linguistic Society of America* 283–340. https://doi.org/10.2307/411155.

Lu, Louis Y. Y., Chih-Hung Hsieh, and John S. Liu. 2016. Development Trajectory and Research Themes of Foresight. *Technological Forecasting and Social Change* 112:347–356. https://doi.org/10.1016/j.techfore.2016.07.040.

Marshakova, Irina. 1973. System of Document Connections Based on References. *Nauchno-Tekhnicheskaya Informatsiya Seriya* 2:3–8.

Marshakova, Irina. 1981. Citation Networks in Information Science. Scientometrics 3. Akadémiai Kiadó, co-published with Springer Science+Business Media B.V., Formerly Kluwer Academic Publishers B.V.: 13–25. https://doi.org/10.1007/bf02021861.

Masini, Eleonora. 1993. *Why Futures Studies?* London, England: Grey Seal.

Mongeon, Philippe, and Adèle Paul-Hus. 2016. The Journal Coverage of Web of Science and Scopus: A Comparative Analysis. *Scientometrics* 106:213–228. https://doi.org/10.1007/s11192-015-1765-5.

Osareh, Farideh. 1996a. Bibliometrics, Citation Analysis and Co-Citation Analysis: A Review of Literature I. *Libri* 46:149–158.

Osareh, Farideh. 1996b. Bibliometrics, Citation Analysis and Co-Citation Analysis: A Review of Literature II. *Libri* 46:217–225.

Prell, Christina. 2012. *Social Network Analysis: History, Theory & Methodology.* Los Angeles, London, New Delhi, Singapore: Sage.

Schulz, Markus S. 2011. The Values of Global Futures. *Current Sociology* 59:268–272. https://doi.org/10.1177/0011392110391163.

Schulz, Markus S. 2015. Future Moves: Forward-Oriented Studies of Culture, Society, and Technology. *Current Sociology* 63:129–139. https://doi.org/10.1177/0011392114556573.

Schulz, Markus S. 2016. Debating Futures: Global Trends, Alternative Visions, and Public Discourse. *International Sociology* 31:3–20. https://doi.org/10.1177/0268580915612941.

Schwartz, Peter. 1997. *Art of the Long View: Planning for the Future in an Uncertain World.* 1st ed. Chichester Weinheim: Wiley.

Scott, John. 2017. *Social Network Analysis.* 4th ed. Los Angeles, London, New Delhi, Singapore: SAGE.

Small, Henry. 1973. Co-citation in the Scientific Literature: A New Measure of the Relationship Between Two Documents. *Journal of the American Society for Information Science* 24:265–269. https://doi.org/10.1002/asi.4630240406.

Small, Henry. 1980. Co-citation Context Analysis and the Structure of Paradigms. *Journal of Documentation* 36:183–196. https://doi.org/10.1108/eb026695.

Tennant, Jonathan P. 2020. Web of Science and Scopus are Not Global Databases of Knowledge. *European Science Editing* 46:e51987. https://doi.org/10.3897/ese.2020.e51987.

Tijssen, Robert J. W., and Anthony F. J. Van Raan. 1994. Mapping Changes in Science and Technology: Bibliometric Co-Occurrence Analysis of the R&D Literature. *Evaluation Review* 18:98–115. https://doi.org/10.1177/0193841X9401800110.

Trowler, Paul, Murray Saunders, and Veronica Bamber, eds. 2012. *Tribes and Territories in the 21st-Century: Rethinking the Significance of Disciplines in Higher Education*. London; New York: Routledge.

Waltman, Ludo, Nees Jan van Eck, and Ed C. M. Noyons. 2010. A Unified Approach to Mapping and Clustering of Bibliometric Networks. *Journal of Informetrics* 4:629–635. https://doi.org/10.1016/j.joi.2010.07.002.

Xu, Linhong, Kun Ding, and Yuan Lin. 2022. Do negative citations reduce the impact of cited papers? *Scientometrics* 127:1161–1186. https://doi.org/10.1007/s11192-021-04214-4.

Yang, Song, Franziska B. Keller, and Lu Zheng. 2017. *Social Network Analysis: Methods and Examples*. Thousand Oaks (CA): Sage Publications.

CHAPTER 5

Epistemic Tribes and Territories in Futures Studies

Abstract This chapter presents and discusses the results of two scientometric analyses of the data on the knowledge collective of futures studies. The two analyses explore two aspects of the attention space: co-citation analysis is used to describe the intellectual lineages, and thus, the epistemic tribes that characterize the attention space, while co-occurrence analysis uses dyads of keywords to describe the research topics, and thus, the epistemic territories claimed by the tribes.

Keywords Co-citation analysis • Co-occurrence analysis • Attention space • Scientometrics • Sociology of science

Introduction

As described in Chap. 2, the origins of futures studies as a scientific endeavor are to be found in the "West." Europeans like H. G. Wells and Ossip K. Flechtheim called for the creation of futurology as an academic discipline, and researchers in North America, among them luminaries like Olaf Helmer or Herman Kahn, contributed the field's first genuine methods (Keßler 2007, 2011; Aligica and Herritt 2009; Gordon 2011; Ghamari-Tabrizi 2005). Yet, at the same time, futures studies proponents had always been convinced that the future is a global issue, and therefore,

© The Author(s), under exclusive license to Springer Nature Switzerland AG 2025
C. Dayé, *Futures Thinking*,
https://doi.org/10.1007/978-3-031-91941-1_5

the attempts at institutionalizing futures studies had been international from very early on (Son 2015; Andersson 2018). With the main channels of scientific communication (conferences, associations, etc.) open to contributions from across the globe, the proponents quickly became aware of the biased nature of futures studies' foundational ideas. Until today, most organizations conducting futures studies put a high priority on international collaboration as a means of increasing the applicability of their research endeavors (Miller 2018). Claims for an inclusive, yet culturally sensitive organization of futures studies were framed as propagating a precondition for increasing the global intellectual relevance of the thus produced images of the future that it produces (Sardar 1993; Bisht 2017).

But what are the current epistemic tribes in futures studies, and which territories do they occupy? What lineages of ideas determine their attention space, and which topics shape it? Following the theoretical frame and the research design introduced in the preceding chapter, this chapter takes an empirical approach to explore structures and characteristics of the attention space of futures studies.

Epistemic Tribes in Futures Studies: Results and Discussion

In Scopus, the search string used to operationalize the knowledge collective of futures tribes—Article title OR Abstract OR Keywords = "futures research" OR "futures studies" OR "futurology"—delivered 13,413 results. From these, VOSviewer retrieved a total of 528,632 references that can be used in a co-citation analysis. However, in order to keep the network mapping readable, not all works can be included. Therefore, those works that have been cited at least sixteen times and showed a total link strength higher than two were selected. This resulted in a network that comprises thirty-five nodes. The "oldest" node, *The Year 2000* by Herman Kahn and Anthony J. Wiener (1967), was published in 1967, while the "youngest," an article on "Designing an experiential scenario" by Stuart Candy and Jake Dunagan (2017), appeared fifty years later. There is one work which has been cited much more often than all the others: Wendell Bell's (1997) two-volume *Foundations of Futures Studies*, which was cited no less than 315 times in the 13,000 articles exported from the database (see the tables below for further details). The next nodes in terms of citation count, Schwartz's *Art of the Long View* (Schwartz 1997) and van der Heijden's *Scenarios* (van der Heijden 1996), received around 100 citations. Bell's book has a total link strength of 448, meaning it was co-cited 448 times together with one of the other nodes entering the network.

The centrality of Bell's books in futures studies' attention space is also represented in the visual display derived from the co-citation analysis (see Fig. 5.1), by both the size of the node and its position in the center of the network. All nodes are allocated according to their proximities, meaning that a node has more co-citation relations with those in its immediate surrounding.

In the network graph, nodes have different colors to denote their belonging to different clusters. What is already clear at first sight is that there is no fragmentation between the clusters. The network comprises nodes that are highly inter-related. While the clustering procedure implemented in VOSviewer's co-citation analysis resulted in five clusters—our epistemic tribes—, these clusters heavily overlap. It is a highly inter-related network without structural holes or bridges (Burt 1992) or anything resembling "weak ties" (Granovetter 1973, 1983).

Now, what are the epistemic tribes in futures studies? Answering this question requires some background knowledge of the literature under scrutiny, and the following are thus my personal interpretations of the things that the various references clustered by the VOSviewer algorithm may share. I decided for the following labels:

- Epistemic tribe #1: Engaging in critical self-reflection (red)
- Epistemic tribe #2: Proposing methodological frameworks (green)
- Epistemic tribe #3: Exploring popular images of the future (blue)
- Epistemic tribe #4: Using scenarios in strategic planning (yellow)
- Epistemic tribe #5: Stabilizing a disciplinary core (purple)

Epistemic tribe #1 sees its lineages to relate to publications that all reflected on the state, functions, tasks, and potentials of futures studies (see Table 5.1). With a periodization that is strikingly similar to Elke Seefried's (2014), Hyeonju Son (2015) explored the intellectual traditions in Western futures studies over three periods. The paper argues that due to the experienced futility of large-scale societal planning efforts and the increased dominance of neoliberal ideologies and practices, futures studies were experiencing an identity crisis. Similar motives inform the two pieces by Ziauddin Sardar. We were living in an "in-between period where old orthodoxies are dying, new ones have not yet emerged, and

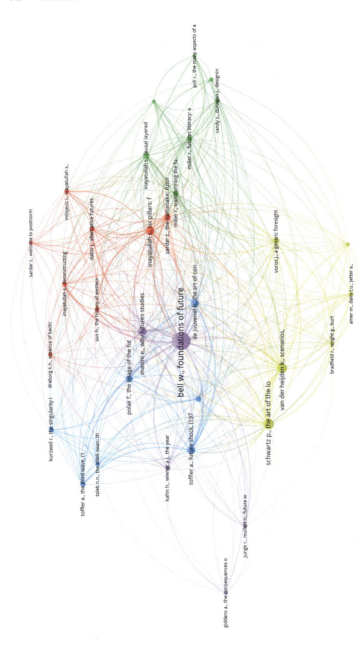

Fig. 5.1 Co-citation network of futures studies

Table 5.1 The first co-citation cluster in futures studies

Epistemic tribe #1: Engaging in critical self-reflection

Source	Freq.	Link strength
Inayatullah S., six pillars: futures thinking for transforming, foresight, 10, 1, pp. 4–21, (2008)	73	113
Sardar Z., the name sake: futures	48	121
Dator J., alternative futures at the manoa school, journal of futures studies, 14, 2, pp. 1–18, (2009)	28	84
Inayatullah S., deconstructing and reconstructing the future: predictive, cultural and critical epistemologies, futures, 22, 2, pp. 115–141, (1990)	23	84
Milojevic I., Inayatullah S., narrative foresight, futures, 73, pp. 151–162, (2015)	23	45
Son H., the history of western futures studies: an exploration of the intellectual traditions and three-phase periodization, futures, 66, pp. 120–137, (2015)	18	80
Dreborg K.H., essence of backcasting, futures, 28, 9, pp. 813–828, (1996)	18	27
Sardar Z., welcome to postnormal times, futures, 42, 5, pp. 435–444, (2010)	16	26

nothing really makes sense," Sardar wrote in "Welcome to postnormal times" (Sardar 2010b, 435), and in "The Namesake" (Sardar 2010a), he offered principles for moving ahead despite the imponderabilia of late modernity (Sardar's four laws of futures studies). Reflecting on how futures studies might find itself a place in the changed environment of late modernity, Soheil Inayatullah (2008) and Jim Dator (2009) both elaborated on the importance of thinking in alternatives in futures studies. Works that trace their intellectual descent to these works are likely to engage in some form of critical reflection about the state—and future—of futures studies.

Related, but still discernible, epistemic tribe #2 is concerned with proposing methodological frameworks for foresight (see Table 5.2). Important intellectual points of reference of this tribe are Inayatullah's (1998) Causal Layered Analysis (CLA), Riel Miller's publications on futures literacy (Miller 2007, 2018), the concept of experiential futures (Candy and Dunagan 2017), or the exploration of the role of speculation in futures and design thinking (Dunne and Raby 2013). Roberto Poli's distinction between anticipation as an empirical phenomenon and the conditions that

Table 5.2 The second co-citation cluster in futures studies

Epistemic tribe #2: Proposing methodologies frameworks

Source	Freq.	Link strength
Inayatullah S., causal layered analysis: poststructuralism as method, futures, 30, 8. pp. 815–829, (1998)	43	92
Miller R., futures literacy: a hybrid strategic scenario method, futures, 39, 4, pp. 341–362, (2007)	31	77
Miller R., transforming the future: anticipation in the twenty-first century, (2018)	31	67
Candy S., Dunagan J., designing an experiential scenario: the people who vanished, futures, 86, pp. 136–153, (2017)	21	40
Dunne A., Raby F., speculative everything: design, fiction, and social dreaming, (2013)	19	27
Slaughter R.A., futures beyond dystopia: creating social foresight, (2004)	17	37
Poli R., the many aspects of anticipation, foresight, 12, 3, pp. 7–17, (2010)	17	29

enable systems to engage in anticipation is also an important source. Members of this epistemic tribe emphasize the lineage of their ideas to these works to corroborate the rootedness and relevance of their own methodological proposals.

A third epistemic tribe assembles around the exploration of popular accounts of the future and of futures thinking (see Table 5.3). Here, we find best-selling books like Alvin Toffler's *Future Shock* (Toffler 1970), Ray Kurzweil's *The Singularity is Near* (Kurzweil 2005), or Nicholas Taleb's *The Black Swan* (Taleb 2007). We also find two early classics of futures studies, Bertrand de Jouvenel's *The Art of Conjecture* (Jouvenel 1967) and Fred L. Polak's *The Image of the Future* (Polak 1973). This makes it plausible to assume that this epistemic tribe is interested in exploring how images of the future are justified, shared, and evaluated in particular cultural environments.

The fourth epistemic tribe in futures studies concentrates on the use of scenario techniques in a variety of settings, but mostly with an interest in enabling forward-looking decision-making (see Table 5.4).

The fifth and final epistemic tribe inhabiting the attention space of futures studies is concerned with stabilizing futures studies as a discipline (see Table 5.5). It emphasizes the field's descent from scientific minds like

Table 5.3 The third co-citation cluster in futures studies

Epistemic tribe #3: Exploring popular images of the future

Source	Freq.	Link strength
de Jouvenel B., the art of conjecture, (1967)	60	143
Toffler A., future shock, (1970)	60	160
Polak F., the image of the future, (1973)	45	112
Bishop P., Hines A., Collins T., the current state of scenario development: an overview of techniques, foresight, 9, 1, pp. 5–25, (2007)	31	90
Toffler A., the third wave, (1980)	29	91
Kurzweil R., the singularity is near: when humans transcend biology, (2005)	25	37
Taleb N.N., the black swan: the impact of the highly improbable, (2007)	18	62

Table 5.4 The fourth co-citation cluster in futures studies

Epistemic tribe #4: Using scenarios in strategic planning

Source	Freq.	Link strength
Schwartz P., the art of the long view	105	195
van der Heijden K., scenarios, the art of strategic conversation	94	184
Voros J., a generic foresight process framework, foresight, 5, 3, pp. 10–21, (2003)	40	86
Amer M., Daim T.U., Jetter A., a review of scenario planning, futures, 46, pp. 23–40, (2013)	21	44
Bradfield R., Wright G., Burt G., Cairns G., van der Heijden K., the origins and evolution of scenario techniques in long range business planning, futures, 37, 8, pp. 795–812. (2005)	20	59
Ramirez R., Selin C., plausibility and probability in scenario planning, foresight, 16, 1, pp. 54–74, (2014)	17	41

Table 5.5 The fifth co-citation cluster in futures studies

Epistemic tribe #5: Stabilizing a disciplinary core

Source	Freq.	Link strength
Bell W., foundations of futures studies	315	448
Masini E., why futures studies?	78	183
Kahn H., Wiener A.J., the year 2000: a framework for speculation on the next thirty-three years, (1967)	26	72
Jungk R., Mullert N., future workshops: how to create desirable futures, (1987)	19	35
Giddens A., the consequences of modernity, (1990)	18	21

Herman Kahn (Kahn and Wiener 1967), without neglecting its active and creative stance and its endorsement of "small democracy" as a path toward socially fair and robust solutions (Jungk and Müllert 1983). But most importantly, of course, they all relate back to the seminal attempt to provide a theoretically stable basis for futures studies as a scientific discipline, Wendell Bell's *Foundations of Futures Studies*. The inclusion of sociologist Anthony Giddens's book on *The Consequences of Modernity* (Giddens 1990) can also be interpreted against this overall thrust of this epistemic tribe to link up with and gain recognition from well-established disciplines within academia.

While certainly not all works fit this interpretation of the clusters neatly, it, nonetheless, seems justified to say that, by and large, the clustering can be meaningfully interpreted. In addition, we can also conclude that the high amount of relations (edges) across the boundaries of the various epistemic tribes indicates that futures studies are not fragmented into smaller, unrelated compartments, as some other social sciences are. Rather, the various epistemic tribes show a considerably high degree of mutual awareness and engagement with the ideas of others. Also, we can note that the clusters themselves do not represent "centers" in a geographical or "scientific school" sense—they are more plausibly interpreted in thematic or substantive than in geographical terms, and all clusters consist of works by a diverse range of authors.

Epistemic Territories in Futures Studies: Results and Discussion

A second option to explore the attention space of the knowledge collective of futures studies (as it is described through the 13,413 publications retrieved from the Scopus database) focuses on the keywords provided by the authors. As argued in the preceding chapter, keywords can be used to explore the dominant topics of an attention space, and thus the epistemic territories claimed by the tribes that inhibit this space.

In total, the data set included 21,354 keywords. Setting a minimum threshold of thirty occurrences resulted in a list of sixty-seven keywords. From these, the three keywords used in the search prompt were removed: "futures studies" (339 occurrences, link strength 269), "futurology" (125 occurrences, link strength 75), and "futures research" (103 occurrences, link strength 80). Further, as futures studies methods have increasingly been used as consensus or planning techniques in medical and nursing studies, the database also included a series of diseases which due to their missing relation to the core interests of futures studies, were also not considered for the network.[1]

The clustering in VOSviewer delivered five clusters, which received the following labels:

- Epistemic territory 1: Public health and the quality of life (red)
- Epistemic territory 2: Climate change and sustainable transformation (green)
- Epistemic territory 3: Foresight and decision-making (blue)
- Epistemic territory 4: Life in the COVID-19 pandemic and after (yellow)
- Epistemic territory 5: The revolutionary potential of digital innovations (purple)

A territory of considerable relevance, thus, is the use of futures studies to address questions of public health and the quality of life. A second epistemic territory relates to efforts around the globe toward sustainable transformation. A third territory is interested in the use of foresight in organizational decision-making. A fourth territory claimed by the futures studies tribes is life during the COVID-19 pandemic and after, whereas a fifth major topic are the potentials and disruptions possibly caused by the advent of artificial intelligence and machine learning (Table 5.6).

---

[1] This concerned the following terms: cancer (113 occurrences, link strength 62), treatment (81 occurrences, link strength 42), immunotherapy (73 occurrences, link strength 34), inflammation (70 occurrences, link strength 28), review (64 occurrences, link strength 34), depression (58 occurrences, link strength 13), chemotherapy (48 occurrences, link strength 31), clinical trials (47 occurrences, link strength 29), biomarkers (45 occurrences, link strength 40), obesity (43 occurrences, link strength 25), drug delivery (43 occurrences, link strength 18), cardiovascular disease (41 occurrences, link strength 27), diabetes (41 occurrences, link strength 25), tissue engineering (39 occurrences, link strength 7), heart failure (38 occurrences, link strength 25), stroke (38 occurrences, link strength 24), breast cancer (38 occurrences, link strength 20), Alzheimer's disease (36 occurrences, link strength 20), hypertension (35 occurrences, link strength 30), lung cancer (34 occurrences, link strength 17), therapy (33 occurrences, link strength 24), HIV (31 occurrences, link strength 21), prostate cancer (31 occurrences, link strength 15), and pregnancy (31 occurrences, link strength 14).

Table 5.6 The co-occurrence clusters of futures studies

Keyword	Frequency	Link strength
Epistemic territory 1: Public health and the quality of life		
Future	96	55
Epidemiology	68	34
Education	64	40
Prevention	53	38
Diagnosis	45	36
Quality of life	44	19
History	41	24
Research	39	20
Ethics	36	26
Genetics	35	14
Public health	35	18
Prognosis	32	27
Screening	31	13
Science fiction	30	32
Training	30	8
Epistemic territory 2: Climate change and sustainable transformation		
Foresight	118	144
Climate change	79	36
Forecasting	62	66
Scenario planning	61	71
Sustainability	54	50
Uncertainty	42	48
Sustain, development	40	45
Future studies	34	20
Strategic planning	32	45
Epistemic territory 3: Foresight and decision making		
Scenarios	69	88
Futures	54	52
Innovation	45	48
Technology	34	26
Causal layered anal.	30	32
Policy	30	25
Epistemic territory 4: Life in the COVID-19 pandemic and after		
Covid-19	152	94
Sars-cov-2	43	45
Gene therapy	42	18
Telemedicine	36	25
Nanotechnology	33	18
Therapy	33	24

(*continued*)

Table 5.6 (continued)

Keyword	Frequency	Link strength
Epistemic territory 5: The revolutionary potential of digital innovations		
Artificial intelligence	112	66
Machine learning	59	35
Tissue engineering	39	7
Deep learning	30	42

A standard way to map the resulting network proceeds by using colors to indicate the clusters, as it was done for the epistemic tribes (see Fig. 5.1). For co-occurrence analyses, VOSviewer also produces network graphs that use colors to indicate the point in time over the last ten years when the keyword was used the most. This visualization format is called overlay visualization (see Fig. 5.2).

What can be thus seen is that, perhaps not surprisingly, the topics receiving the most attention over the last years by futures studies' authors either concerned the COVID-19 pandemic or recent advances in digital technologies, in particular artificial intelligence and machine learning. Other topics, for example, prevention, quality of life, or ethics, remained important, but less so than in the early 2010s. Compared to forecasting, foresight became a more "modern" term, and the same holds true if one compares future to futures.

Conclusion

Based on the research design followed in this book, we can now say that the attention space of futures studies can be characterized, on the one hand, by five dominant epistemic tribes that are concerned with different intellectual projects. Epistemic tribe #1 conducts a critical self-reflection about the form, functions, and tasks of futures studies. Epistemic tribe #2 develops broad methodological frameworks and programs to ensure a healthy future for the field, whereas epistemic tribe #3 is more interested in questioning widely shared images of the future. Epistemic tribe #4 promotes the use of scenarios in strategic planning, and epistemic tribe #5 sets as its objective to stabilize futures studies as an academic discipline. Of course, these interpretations are conjectures, but these conjectures align with the empirical results.

80 C. DAYÉ

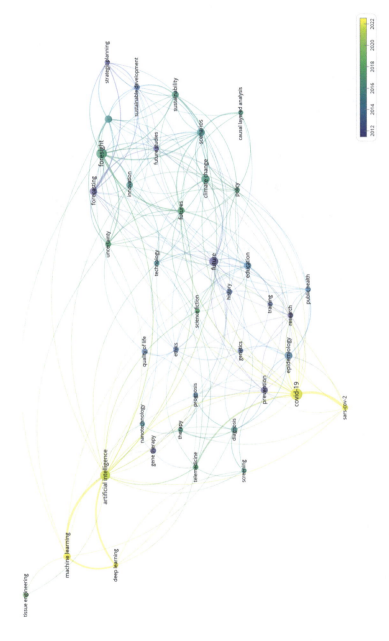

Fig. 5.2 Overlay visualization of futures studies' epistemic territories

As regards the epistemic territories claimed by these tribes, that is, the topics that their publications address, five seem to have been dominating: public health, sustainability, anticipatory decision-making, the COVID-19 pandemic, and innovations in digital technologies.

References

Aligica, P. D., and R. Herritt. 2009. Epistemology, Social Technology, and Expert Judgement: Olaf Helmer's Contribution to Futures Research. *Futures* 41:253–259. https://doi.org/10.1016/j.futures.2008.11.010.

Andersson, Jenny. 2018. *The Future of the World: Futurology, Futurists, and the Struggle for the Post Cold War Imagination*. Oxford, New York: Oxford University Press.

Bell, Wendell. 1997. *Foundations of Futures Studies*. 2 vols. Human Science for a New Era. New Brunswick, NJ: Transaction Publishers.

Bisht, Pupul. 2017. *Decolonizing Futures: Exploring Storytelling as a Tool for Inclusion in Foresight*. MA thesis, Toronto, ON: OCAD University.

Burt, Ronald S. 1992. *Structural Holes: The Social Structure of Competition*. Cambridge (MA), London: Harvard University Press.

Candy, Stuart, and Jake Dunagan. 2017. Designing an Experiential Scenario: The People Who Vanished. *Futures* 86:136–153. https://doi.org/10.1016/j.futures.2016.05.006.

Dator, Jim. 2009. Alternative Futures at the Manoa School. *Journal of Futures Studies* 14:1–18.

Dunne, Anthony, and Fiona Raby. 2013. *Speculative Everything: Design, Fiction, and Social Dreaming*. Cambridge (MA), London: The MIT Press.

Ghamari-Tabrizi, Sharon. 2005. *The Worlds of Herman Kahn. The Intuitive Science of Thermonuclear War*. Cambridge (MA), London: Harvard University Press.

Giddens, Anthony. 1990. *The Consequences of Modernity*. Stanford (CA): Stanford University Press.

Gordon, Theodore J. 2011. Obituary - Olaf Helmer, Futures Thinker. *Technological Forecasting and Social Change* 78:1099–1100.

Granovetter, Mark S. 1973. The Strength of Weak Ties. *American Journal of Sociology* 78:1360–1380.

Granovetter, Mark S. 1983. The Strength of Weak Ties: A Network Theory Revisited. *Sociological Theory* 1:201–233.

van der Heijden, Kees. 1996. *Scenarios: The Art of Strategic Conversation*. Chichester: Wiley.

Inayatullah, Sohail. 1998. Causal Layered Analysis. *Futures* 30:815–829. https://doi.org/0016-3287/98.

Inayatullah, Sohail. 2008. Six pillars: Futures Thinking for Transforming. *Foresight* 10:4–21. https://doi.org/10.1108/14636680810855991.

Jouvenel, Bertrand de. 1967. *The Art of Conjecture*. New York: Basic Books.
Jungk, Robert, and Norbert R. Müllert. 1983. *Zukunftswerkstätten. Wege zur Wiederbelebung der Demokratie*. München: Goldmann.
Kahn, Herman, and Anthony J. Wiener. 1967. *The Year 2000: A Framework for Speculation on the Next Thirty-three Years*. Macmillan.
Keßler, Mario. 2007. *Ossip K. Flechtheim: politischer Wissenschaftler und Zukunftsdenker (1909–1998)*. Köln: Böhlau.
Keßler, Mario. 2011. Zur Futurologie von Ossip K. Flechtheim. In *Macht und Geist im Kalten Krieg*, ed. Bernd Greiner, Tim B. Müller, and Claudia Weber, 239–257. Hamburg: Hamburger Edition.
Kurzweil, Ray. 2005. *The Singularity Is Near: When Humans Transcend Biology*. 1st ed. New York: Viking.
Miller, Riel. 2007. Futures Literacy: A Hybrid Strategic Scenario Method. *Futures* 39:341–362. https://doi.org/10.1016/j.futures.2006.12.001.
Miller, Riel, ed. 2018. *Transforming the Future: Anticipation in the 21st Century*. Routledge.
Polak, Fred L. 1973. *The Image of the Future*. Translated by Elise Boulding. Amsterdam, London, New York: Elsevier.
Sardar, Ziauddin. 1993. Colonizing the Future: The 'Other' Dimension of Futures Studies. *Futures* 25:179–187. https://doi.org/10.1016/0016-3287(93)90163-N.
Sardar, Ziauddin. 2010a. The Namesake: Futures; Futures Studies; Futurology; Futuristic; Foresight—What's in a Name? *Futures* 42:177–184. https://doi.org/10.1016/j.futures.2009.11.001.
Sardar, Ziauddin. 2010b. Welcome to Postnormal Times. *Futures* 42:435–444. https://doi.org/10.1016/j.futures.2009.11.028.
Schwartz, Peter. 1997. *Art of the Long View: Planning for the Future in an Uncertain World*. 1st ed. Chichester Weinheim: Wiley.
Seefried, Elke. 2014. Steering the Future. The Emergence of "Western" Futures Research and Its Production of Expertise, 1950s to Early 1970s. *European Journal of Futures Research* 2:12 pages. https://doi.org/10.1007/s40309-013-0029-y.
Son, Hyeonju. 2015. The History of Western Futures Studies: An Exploration of the Intellectual Traditions and Three-Phase Periodization. *Futures* 66:120–137. https://doi.org/10.1016/j.futures.2014.12.013.
Taleb, Nassim Nicholas. 2007. *The Black Swan: The Impact of the Highly Improbable*. 1st ed. Random House.
Toffler, Alvin. 1970. *Future Shock*. New York: Random House.

CHAPTER 6

Epistemic Tribes and Territories in the Sociology of the Future

Abstract After establishing that there indeed exists a body of sociological literature concerned with futures thinking, this chapter presents and discusses the results of the two scientometric procedures used in this book to describe the attention space of the sociology of the future. Like Chap. 5 did for futures studies, co-citation analysis is used to describe the epistemic tribes that characterize the attention space of the sociology of the future, while co-occurrence analysis is used to describe the research topics, and thus, the epistemic territories claimed by these tribes. In the conclusion, the findings for the two bodies of literature are compared.

Keywords Co-citation analysis • Co-occurrence analysis • Attention space • Scientometrics • Sociology of science

Introduction

A second, perhaps less obvious place to look for social scientific futures thinking is the sociology of the future. This sub-field has not (yet) seen much academic institutionalization. While soon after its foundation in 1949, the International Sociological Association (ISA) established a Research Committee on Futures Research (RC07; see Chap. 2), this initiative has not transpired to other professional organizations—for instance, there is no comparable section in the American Sociological Association (ASA) or in its British, French, or German counterparts. Also, it is hard to find indications of something resembling a canonization, as there are no dedicated textbooks or other didactic sources available.

The research design used in the preceding chapter for futures studies literature can nonetheless be used for sociology, too—under the condition that there is such a thing as the sociology of the future. Thus, in a first step, this chapter turns to establishing the phenomenon: Do sociologists concern themselves with futures? Having shown that they indeed do, the chapter proceeds with the analysis of the epistemic tribes in the sociology of the future and the territories that they claim.

Using the identical research procedure allows for comparing the results for futures studies and the sociology of the future. This comparison is of utmost interest, in particular, regarding the third research question that concerns the intellectual and theoretical sources. The most pressing question in terms of the organization of futures thinking in the social sciences is whether we are dealing with one large, two linked, or two (or more) separate attention spaces. These and related issues will be discussed in conclusion.

Establishing the Phenomenon: Future(s) in Sociology

Is it possible to find among sociologist a deep interest in the future? In other words, one that goes beyond the fundamental future orientation of all science, as manifested in the concept of the progress of knowledge?

As described in Chap. 4, the data used to describe the attention space of the sociology of the future consisted of all articles that included "future" or "futures" in their title and were published in journals that included the term "sociolog*" in their name. If we take, in a first step, simply the frequency distribution of such articles over time as an indicator of sociological interest, we find—in absolute figures—a continuously rising curve (see Fig. 6.1).

Of course, this is not very meaningful on its own when you consider that sociological publication activity as a whole is likely to have increased steadily—especially that which is recorded in digital databases such as Scopus. It is therefore important to put these figures in relation to the

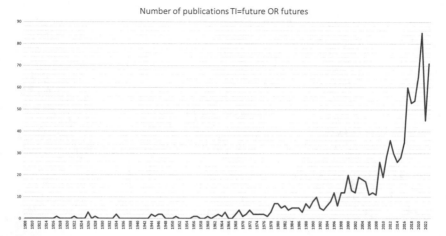

Fig. 6.1 Frequency of terms "future" and "futures" in titles of articles published in sociological journals, 1908–2023 (N = 988)

total output of the journals covered by the search query. This was achieved by carrying out the same search query in Scopus without the part after the AND, that is, without the restriction to those articles with "future" or "futures" in the title: Source Title (SO) = sociolog*. This search query returned 119,409 hits, spread over the years from 1908 to 2023. The two values now available can be used to determine what percentage of all articles published in a given year had the terms "future" or "futures" in the title.

A line chart limited to the period from 1970 for the sake of clarity (see Fig. 6.2) supports the thesis that interest in the future has grown within sociology in recent decades. Although it is still a fragile little plant—the percentages range from approximately 0.15% to 1.5%—the trend is at least pointing upwards.

The first research question can therefore be answered: sociology is increasingly thinking about futures. The topic is by no means booming, but it has enjoyed growing attention over the last five decades.

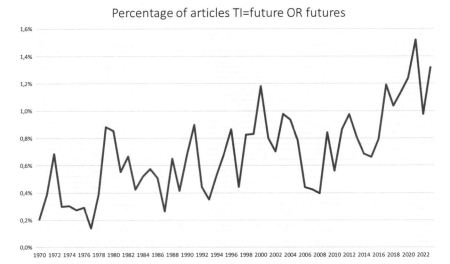

Fig. 6.2 Share (in %) of articles with terms "future" or "futures" in the title among the overall output in sociological journals

Epistemic Tribes in the Sociology of the Future: Results and Discussion

What epistemic tribes can be found in the attention space of the sociology of the future? What are central points of reference, from which the ideas discussed in the publications draw inspiration and corroboration? What are important sources in sociological futures thinking? These questions can be addressed by a co-citation analysis. Co-citation analyses determine how often two sources are mentioned together in the bibliographies of the articles examined, that is, how often a particular dyad occurs. These frequencies then determine both the proximity to other nodes and the strength of the edge.

Using a threshold of 13 as the minimum number of citations, VOSViewer produces a network comprising 37 nodes and orders it into three clusters (see Fig. 6.3).

Similar to the co-citation network that resulted for the attention space of futures studies, we also find for the sociology of the future that one node by far exceeds all others in importance. In this case, it is Ulrich Beck's (1986; English 1992) book *Risk Society*, which is the most cited source with forty-four citations. In second to fifth place are Anne Mische's (2009) article on "Projects and Possibilities" in *Sociological Forum*

6 EPISTEMIC TRIBES AND TERRITORIES IN THE SOCIOLOGY OF THE FUTURE 87

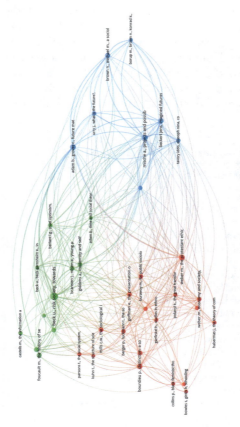

Fig. 6.3 Co-citation network of the sociology of the future

(twenty-eight citations), Barbara Adam and Chris Groves's (2007) book *Future Matters* (twenty-six citations), Max Weber's essay on Protestant ethics and the spirit of capitalism (also twenty-six citations) and Jens Beckert's (2013) essay "Imagined Futures" in *Theory & Society* (twenty-five citations).

In comparison to other co-citation networks—including the futures studies network described in Chap. 5—it can be observed that the clusters are relatively clearly differentiated in terms of location. Further, the clusters are not separated: almost all nodes also have edges to nodes in other clusters. This allows the interpretation that the three clusters correspond to directions of thought or research that are relatively stable in themselves, without being separated from other, thematically similar directions (Tables 6.1 and 6.2).

Table 6.1 The first co-citation cluster in the sociology of the future

Epistemic tribe #1: Analyzing the reproduction of social inequalities

Source	Freq.	Link strength
Weber M., the protestant ethic and the spirit of capitalism, (1976)	26	71
Bourdieu P., distinction: a social critique of the judgement of taste, (1984)	23	42
Marx K., capital: a critique of political economy. London, (1867)	19	20
Mills C.W., the sociological imagination, (1959)	19	19
Weber M., economy and society, (1918)	18	32
Goffman E., the presentation of self in everyday life, (1959)	18	31
Burawoy M., for public sociology (2004 asa presidential address), American sociological review, 70, 1, pp. 4–28, (2005)	16	18
Berger P., Luckmann T., the social construction of knowledge: a treatise in the sociology of knowledge, (1987)	16	17
Garfinkel H., studies in ethnomethodology, (1967)	15	33
Parsons T., the social system, (1951)	15	17
Polanyi K., the great transformation: The political and economic origins of our time, (1957)	15	15
Durkheim E., the division of labor in society	14	39
Piketty T., capital in the twenty-first century, (2014)	14	21
Habermas J., the theory of communicative action, (1984)	14	17
Lareau A., unequal childhoods: Class, race, and family life, (2003)	13	19
Bowles S, Gintis H, schooling in capitalist America: Educational reform and contradictions of economic life, (1976)	13	11
Collins P., black feminist thought: Knowledge, consciousness, and the politics of empowerment, (1990)	13	10
Kuhn T., the structure of scientific revolutions, (1962)	13	9

Table 6.2 The second co-citation cluster in the sociology of the future

Epistemic tribe #2: Exploring social life in modernity and late modernity

Source	Freq.	Link strength
Beck U., risk society. Towards a new modernity, (1992)	44	108
Adam B., Groves C., future matters, action, knowledge, ethics, (2007)	26	122
Foucault M., the history of sexuality, (1979)	20	20
Foucault M., discipline and punish: The birth of the prison, (1995)	19	39
Giddens A., modernity and self-identity: Self and society in the late modern age, (1991)	18	54
Brannen J., Nilsen A., young people's time perspectives: From youth to adulthood, sociology, 6, 3, pp. 513–537, (2002)	18	43
Giddens A., consequences of modernity, (1990)	17	49
Berlant L.G., cruel optimism, (2011)	14	39
Castells M., the information age volume i: The rise of network society, (1996)	14	10
Beck U., Beck-Gernsheim E., individualization: Institutionalized individualism and its social and political consequences, (2002)	13	28
Foucault M., the birth of biopolitics: Lectures at the college de France 1978–1979, (2008)	13	14

But what do the epistemic tribes thus described stand for? In my view, the following interpretations are appropriate:

- Epistemic tribe #1: Analyzing the reproduction of social inequalities (red)
- Epistemic tribe #2: Exploring social life in modernity and late modernity (green)
- Epistemic tribe #3: Assessing spaces of foresight and agency (blue)

The first epistemic tribe in the sociology of future is concerned with analyzing the reproduction of social inequalities (Table 6.1). Judged from their citation patterns, it traces its decent to sociological classics, ranging from the early trinity Karl Marx (1887; German original 1867), Max Weber (1978; German original 1920; 1992; German original 1905), and Émile Durkheim (1933; French original 1893) to mid-twentieth-century writers such as C. Wright Mills (2000; original 1959), Erving Goffman (1956), Talcott Parsons (1951), Harold Garfinkel (1967), and Peter L. Berger and Thomas Luckmann (1991; original 1966). Capitalism is explored by this tribe as a major driver of social inequalities, in the course of which additional lineages are drawn to Karl Polanyi (1957) and a few more recent contributions.

The second epistemic tribe is exploring social life in the conditions of modernity and late modernity (Table 6.2). Beck's *Risk Society* belongs in this cluster, but philosopher Michel Foucault also plays an important role. Anthony Giddens's studies also continue to be important points of reference (e.g., Giddens 1990).

The final third epistemic tribe governing the attention space of the sociology of the future is interested in assessing the relations between foresight, individual and collective, and agency (Table 6.3). This tribe, for instance, traces its descent to the well-known explorations of the dynamics of expectations in science, technology, and economy (Brown and Michael 2003; Borup et al. 2006; Beckert 2013), but also includes more fundamental explorations from social theory on anticipation as human capacity and its relation to agency (Adam 1990; Emirbayer and Mische 1998; Mische 2009; Tavory and Eliasoph 2013). (Table 6.3).

Table 6.3 The third co-citation cluster in the sociology of the future

Epistemic tribe #3: Assessing spaces of foresight and agency

Source	Freq.	Link strength
Mische A., projects and possibilities: Researching futures in action, sociological forum, 24, pp. 694–704, (2009)	28	103
Beckert Jens, imagined futures: Fictional expectations in the economy, theory and society, 42, 3, pp. 219–240, (2013)	25	98
Brown N., Michael M., a sociology of expectations: Retrospecting prospects and prospecting retrospects, technology analysis & strategic management, 15, 1, pp. 3–18, (2003)	21	66
Emirbayer M., Mische A., what is agency?, american journal of sociology, 103, 4, pp. 962–1023, (1998)	16	68
Tavory I., Eliasoph N., coordinating futures: Toward a theory of anticipation, American journal of sociology, 118, pp. 908–942, (2013)	16	62
Urry J., what is the future?, (2016)	16	53
Borup M., Brown N., Konrad K., van Lente H., the sociology of expectations in science and technology, technology analysis & strategic management, 18, 3–4, pp. 285–298, (2006)	14	47
Adam B., time and social theory, (1990)	13	32

Drawing on the analysis presented in Chap. 5, it is striking that almost none of the sources used in sociology have high citation values in futures studies—and vice versa. Notable exceptions are Barbara Adam and Chris Groves's (2007) book *Future Matters* and Anthony Giddens's (1990) analysis of *The Consequences of Modernity*. Wendell Bell, the ultimate center of futures studies (Bell 1997), does not make it into the lineage, despite his long-term affiliation with the highly esteemed sociology department at Yale University.

What is more, high citation levels are reserved for works by authors who, despite their overarching interests, can be classified as sociologists—exceptions are the ubiquitous Michel Foucault and the literary scholar Lauren Berlant. In addition to the thematic lines of this inquiry, this is probably the most important finding from the study presented in this chapter: sociologists who write about the future primarily refer to texts by other sociologists. Debates, contributions, and insights made within futures studies are not received with the same intensity as intra-disciplinary contributions. And while some caution is appropriate due to the exploratory character of the research presented here, it can, nonetheless, be said that the same appears to hold for futures studies: scholars active in the field are first and foremost using futures studies publications to corroborate their points; and the sources invoked in the sociology of the future to contextualize and corroborate one's claims are by and large neglected.

Epistemic Territories in the Sociology of the Future: Results and Discussion

As explained, the second approach to mapping the attention space of futures studies used in this book relies on a co-occurrence analysis of keywords provided by the authors. In relation to a specific text corpus, a co-occurrence analysis determines with which other words (or lexical units) a word occurs together. If, as in the research design proposed here, the analysis is restricted to the keywords of academic articles, the procedure determines the frequency with which each keyword is mentioned together with others. These resulting co-occurrence relationships are then represented as a network.

With the settings [Co-occurrence; Author keywords; Full counting; Minimum occurrence: 5], VOSViewer delivers a network of fifty nodes—a further 2015 keywords do not exceed the threshold of five mentions and are therefore not considered. In addition, the program determines six clusters (see Table 6.4). These are labelled as follows:

Table 6.4 The co-occurrence clusters of the sociology of the future

Keyword	Frequency	Link strength
Epistemic territory 1: Technology and the future of work		
Education	14	10
Gender	13	18
Future of work	11	11
Family	9	11
Race	8	13
Young people	8	13
Technology	8	6
Racism	7	12
Automation	7	7
Health	5	7
Anthropocene	5	5
Social mobility	5	5
Epistemic territory 2: Globalization and cultural identity		
Youth	14	16
Social movements	11	17
Inequality	10	11
Identity	10	10
Migration	8	14
Globalization	8	8
Intersectionality	8	8
Culture	7	10
Qualitative research	5	4
Mental health	5	3
Transnationalism	5	1
Epistemic territory 3: Capitalism, neoliberalism and democracy		
Future	40	56
Neoliberalism	12	12
Climate change	11	11
Democracy	9	8
Social theory	8	14
Cosmopolitanism	5	10
Capitalism	5	8
New Zealand	5	8
Utopia	5	4
Epistemic territory 4: Expectations and images of the future		
Aspiration	14	29
Class	13	14
Imagined futures	9	14
Higher education	8	5
Agency	6	14

(*continued*)

Table 6.4 (continued)

Keyword	Frequency	Link strength
Expectations	5	13
Imaginaries	5	11
Innovation	5	6
Epistemic territory 5: History and future of sociology		
Sociology	23	15
Social change	12	15
History of sociology	7	9
Ageing	6	1
Sociological theory	5	8
Epistemic territory 6: Sociology of time and the study of risk		
Futures	20	23
Time	14	22
Temporality	14	18
Covid-19	12	11
Risk	7	5

- Epistemic territory 1: Technology and the future of work (red)
- Epistemic territory 2: Globalization and cultural identity (green)
- Epistemic territory 3: Capitalism, neoliberalism, and democracy (blue)
- Epistemic territory 4: Expectations and images of the future (yellow)
- Epistemic territory 5: History and future of sociology (purple)
- Epistemic territory 6: Sociology of time and the study of risk (light blue)

As before, to make it easier to interpret the content, Table 6.4 arranges the keywords according to clusters and, within the clusters, according to their significance (frequency of occurrence, link strength in terms of degree centrality or degree). The link strength indicates with how many other keywords the keyword in question occurs together. A content-related interpretation of the link strength is only possible and meaningful in comparison to other nodes. If we compare "education" (from cluster 1) and "aspiration" (from cluster 4), for example, we can see that both occur equally often in the data corpus, namely, fourteen times. However, "education" occurs in combination with significantly fewer other keywords than "aspiration" (link strength 10 vs. 29). This leads to the conclusion that "education" has a much more precise, narrower scope of application, while "aspiration" is mentioned in many different contexts. An extreme case is "ageing" (cluster 5): the keyword occurs six times (frequency = 6), but of the keywords with which it is mentioned together in the data corpus, only one, namely, "social change," makes it over the hurdle of five mentions (hence link strength = 1).

An analysis of these clusters can begin by pointing out that the tribes within the sociology of the future claim six different epistemic territories. First, they concern themselves with studying the development of technologies and how this impacts the future of work. Second, they address the question of how human beings stabilize their social identities in times marked by globalization, or more precisely, under conditions of global (forced and deliberate) migration and high flexibilities in the labor market. Third, they are critically concerned with how to protect democracy from the distorting effects of capitalism and neoliberal governance.

A fifth epistemic territory in the attention space of the sociology of the future is the history and future of discipline itself. Similar to the epistemic territory in futures studies that reflected on its own changing forms, functions, and tasks, scholars in the sociology of the future also question which social shape, functions, and tasks sociology might take in the future, and they make use of the sociology's past as a discipline to inform this futures thinking. A final and sixth territory to which the sociology of the future makes demands is the sociology of time and the study of risk.

Apart from interpreting and labelling the keyword clusters resulting from co-occurrence analysis, it is also important to ask the counter question: Which territories are not claimed? In particular, as the research design followed here allows for direct comparison: Which topics that are explored in futures studies are not echoed in the sociology of the future?

What immediately jumps the observer's eye is that the topic of technology is treated rather one-sided. Topics like "artificial intelligence" or "machine learning" that made up a separate territory in futures studies do not even appear as keywords, although it can be assumed that such topics are addressed in epistemic territory 1, when it comes to the "future of work" and "automation" or when the reproduction of inequalities and biases by decision-supporting systems is explored (e.g., "racism," "health"). The lack of keywords such as artificial intelligence, surveillance, or facial recognition can also be interpreted to mean that a large number of specialized, interdisciplinary journals are available for these new technology topics. Another topic that is discussed in current futures studies publications, but are missing from the territorial map of the sociology of the future, concerns sustainability.

In line with Chap. 5, an overlay visualization is used to show the network of keywords. Overlay visualization retain the network structure but use the coloring of the nodes to indicate the time of their most frequent occurrence. In VOSViewer, this period is automatically limited to the last ten years, but the result still allows interesting conclusions to be drawn about the shifts that have taken place within the discourse represented by the network.

At the center of the network—and therefore also the largest node—is "future" as the most frequently mentioned keyword. Right next to it we find the plural form "futures." This is somewhat surprising insofar as, according to our search query, at least one of these terms is also mentioned in the title. Experience shows that some authors tend to mention terms in the keywords that are not mentioned in the title, as this increases the likelihood that the article will be captured by search queries. The fact that these terms are nevertheless at the center of the network can be interpreted as an indication that the articles captured by the search query clearly emphasize their future relevance and do not want to be understood as a mere side effect of other analytical steps that are considered more important (e.g., in the sense of an outlook).

As can be seen in Fig. 6.4, the past ten years have seen shifts away from certain keywords toward others across all clusters. Dark blue keywords such as "identity," "globalization," "class," and "health" were chosen more frequently in the 2010s than in the recent past, where yellow keywords such as "covid-19," "anthropocene," "young people," and "agency" were frequently mentioned. Green-colored buzzwords such as "future," "futures," or "climate change" are likely to be consistently popular and therefore fall into the middle category.

What is striking here is that terms associated with an active, constructive, subject-oriented view of the future are consistently in the younger color spectrum: "agency," "expectations," "imaginaries," "imagined futures." Conversely, terms that characterize socio-structural effects—"culture," "globalization," "class," "identity," "risk"—do not seem to be very popular at the moment.

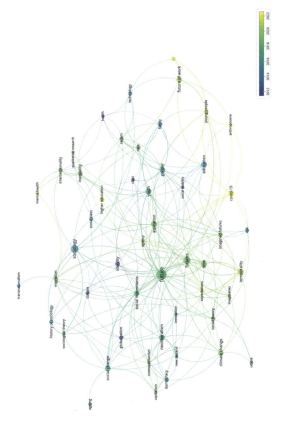

Fig. 6.4 Overlay visualization of epistemic territories in the sociology of the future

Conclusion

Where does this leave us in terms of the overall objective of this book? By and large, we have to conclude that the two knowledge collectives within the social sciences that explicitly concern themselves with producing images of the future—futures studies and the sociology of the future—are separate attention spaces. With a few exceptions, they claim different lineages, that is, they use different sources to contextualize and corroborate their own arguments. Also, it appears that, for the most part, they claim different epistemic territories. Although this would require further analyses, we might formulate the hypothesis that there exists some tacit division of intellectual labor between the two collectives.

This finding is of course not conducive to interdisciplinary dialog. Both disciplines run the risk of becoming entangled in endless debates about questions that the other has already solved. At the same time, however, the finding also provides an indication of possible first steps toward a mutual rapprochement. In order to build a common repertoire, it can be useful to introduce each other to the debates that are considered central within one's own field. Researchers who are familiar with both disciplines and are able to convey the subtle differences in their approaches in a nuanced way can make a name for themselves as translators and bridge builders.

References

Adam, Barbara. 1990. *Time & Social Theory*. Erste Ausgabe Edition. Cambridge: Temple U.
Adam, Barbara, and Chris Groves. 2007. *Future Matters: Action, Knowledge, Ethics*. Leiden: Brill.
Beck, Ulrich. 1986. *Risikogesellschaft. Auf dem Weg in eine andere Moderne*. Frankfurt am Main: Suhrkamp.
Beck, Ulrich. 1992. Risk Society: Towards a New Modernity. Translated by Mark Ritter. London, Newbury Park, New Delhi: Sage Publications.
Beckert, Jens. 2013. Imagined futures: Fictional Expectations in the Economy. *Theory and Society* 42:219–240. https://doi.org/10.1007/s11186-013-9191-2.
Bell, Wendell. 1997. *Foundations of Futures Studies. 2 vols. Human Science for a New Era*. New Brunswick, NJ: Transaction Publishers.
Berger, Peter L., and Thomas Luckmann. 1991. *The Social Construction of Reality. A Treatise in the Sociology of Knowledge*. London: Penguin.
Borup, Mads, Nik Brown, Kornelia Konrad, and Harro Van Lente. 2006. The Sociology of Expectations in Science and Technology. *Technology Analysis & Strategic Management* 18:285–298. https://doi.org/10.1080/09537320600777002.

Brown, Nik, and Mike Michael. 2003. A Sociology of Expectations: Retrospecting Prospects and Prospecting Retrospects. *Technology Analysis & Strategic Management* 15:3–18. https://doi.org/10.1080/0953732032000046024.
Durkheim, Emile. 1933. *The Division of Labor in Society*. Translated by George Simpson. Glencoe, IL: Free Press.
Emirbayer, Mustafa, and Ann Mische. 1998. What Is Agency? *American Journal of Sociology* 103:962–1023. https://doi.org/10.1086/231294.
Garfinkel, Harold. 1967. *Studies in Ethnomethodology*. Englewood Cliffs (NJ): Prentice-Hall.
Giddens, Anthony. 1990. *The Consequences of Modernity*. Stanford (CA): Stanford University Press.
Goffman, Erving. 1956. The Presentation of Self in Everyday Life. In *Social Science Research Centre Monographs 2*. Edinburgh: Doubleday.
Marx, Karl. 1887. *Capital: A Critique of Political Economy. Vol. 1*. Translated by Samuel Moore and Edward Aveling. London.
Mills, C. Wright. 2000. *The Sociological Imagination*. Oxford, New York: Oxford University Press.
Mische, Ann. 2009. Projects and Possibilities: Researching Futures in Action. *Sociological Forum* 24:694–704. https://doi.org/10.1111/j.1573-7861.2009.01127.x.
Parsons, Talcott. 1951. *The Social System*. London: The Free Press of Glencoe.
Polanyi, Karl. 1957. *The Great transformation: The Political and Economic Origins of Our Time*. Boston (MA) Theo: Beacon.
Tavory, Iddo, and Nina Eliasoph. 2013. Coordinating Futures: Toward a Theory of Anticipation. *American Journal of Sociology* 118:908–942. https://doi.org/10.1086/668646
Weber, Max. 1978. Economy and Society: An Outline of Interpretive Sociology. In *Berkeley*, ed. Guenther Roth and Claus Wittich. Los Angeles, London: University of California Press.
Weber, Max. 1992. *The Protestant Ethic and the Spirit of Capitalism*. Edited by Talcott Parsons. London: Routledge.

CHAPTER 7

Conclusion: The Future of Futures Thinking in the Social Sciences

Abstract This last chapter leaves the realms of description and analysis to speculate about the possible trajectories of the two fields in the social sciences that concern themselves with futures thinking, that is, futures studies and the sociology of the future. Based on the empirical studies, it is argued that recent developments in how the sciences are organized—first and foremost characterized by a continued erosion of disciplines—pose a more severe risk to the sociology of the future than to futures studies, as the first shows more characteristics of a discipline than the latter. Yet, ideally, instead of ignoring each other or, worse, ridiculing each other's knowledge claims, an arrangement between the two might be realized that allows for a diligent division of labor. Together, the two fields could achieve a more balanced form of futures thinking that provides answers to urgent societal needs while maintaining the stability of an academic discipline.

Keywords Disciplines • Epistemic hopes • Futures studies • Sociology of the future • Trading zones

INTRODUCTION

According to Socrates in Plato's *Theaetetus*, Thales of Miletus had one day been so lost in thought that he had fallen into a hole. A Thracian woman who was passing by mocked him, exclaiming that while Thales was trying

© The Author(s), under exclusive license to Springer Nature Switzerland AG 2025
C. Dayé, *Futures Thinking*,
https://doi.org/10.1007/978-3-031-91941-1_7

with all his might to understand things in the sky, what was right in front of his feet remained hidden from him. "The same jest," Socrates said according to Plato (Theaetetus, 174a, translation by Harold N. Fowler), "applies to all who pass their lives in philosophy."[1] Until today, the Thracian passerby exemplifies one often-heard allegation toward scientific theorizing (Blumenberg 1987), in particular in the social sciences and humanities: their doings lack benefit, and spinning lofty ideas will not help finding solutions to nagging problems in the world.

Yet, as in any public reputation game, for each allegation exists a counter-allegation. Social scientists and humanities scholars can also be perceived as being too close to the problems of the world, or more precisely, to things that particular groups of people define as problems. "Whose bread I eat, their song I sing"—this proverb can be traced back to writings of Michael Beheim, a fifteenth-century singer wandering through the German lands.[2] The allegation is that science that is too interested in solving problems begins to propose the solutions that profit people in power and wealth. Scientific research, as Robert K. Merton (1996; Panofsky 2010) and others argued, needs to be disinterested, independent from non-scientific considerations, and, in this regard, autonomous.

Researchers in the social sciences and humanities thus have to find ways to avoid being likened to both Thales without risking the Beheim allegation, and vice versa. This is all the more problematic when the knowledge produced concerns the future, just because, as Wendell Bell (2003, 144) put it, this "knowledge of the future" is "the most useful knowledge" we have "[i]n making our way in the world, both individually and collectively." Building on considerations and studies presented in earlier parts of this book, this chapter reflects on how the current institutionalization of futures in the social sciences reflects the various challenges that confront such intellectual endeavor, and speculates about possible future developments.

---

[1] See http://www.perseus.tufts.edu/hopper/text?doc=Perseus%3Atext%3A1999.01.0172%3Atext%3DTheaet.%3Asection%3D174a, accessed 3 January 2025.

[2] The version known today in German speaking areas, "Wes' Brot ich ess', des' Lied ich sing," emerged a bit later. With minor variations, e.g. in the noun, the proverb also exists in other European languages, for example, in Czech (Koho chleba jíš, toho píseň zpívej), Slovenian (Čigar kruh jem, tega pesmi pojem), or Dutch (Wiens brood men eet, diens woord men spreekt). I am grateful to Marek Skovajsa (Prague), Andreas Unterweger (Leibnitz), and George Gussenhoven (Graz) for their support in checking the translations.

Thales, Beheim, and the Challenges of Scientific Futures Thinking

The motif that it was science's task to deliver knowledge about the future already ran through classical utopias, for example, in Francis Bacon's *New Atlantis*, and found expression in the work of (proto-) sociologists in the early nineteenth century, above all, of course, in the work of Auguste Comte who famously stated that from science comes foresight, and from foresight action ("science, d'où prévoyance; prévoyance, d'où action"; Auguste Comte, *Cours de philosophie positive*, deuxième leçon).

This tenet, of course, puts science in a comfortable position, as it suggest a direct social benefit of science that is easy to communicate: paraphrasing Comte, one could say that science provides the knowledge about the future that makes prosperous social decision-making possible in the first place. Knowledge enables foresight, and foresight empowers us to take social action. But "foreknowledge" is fundamentally at odds with the claims to knowledge that have become the consensus in the cultural areas that have shaped (or dominated) the sciences in recent centuries: that knowledge claims can be empirically verified, and even more: that they must already be empirically verified at the time of their public expression. How can scientific knowledge about the future be generated without simultaneously disregarding the self-imposed definition of knowledge and thus ultimately undermining the social function of science as a whole?

In addition to the difficulty that scientific images of the future cannot be directly verified or refuted at the time they are made, but can at most be confirmed or supported, there are further methodological difficulties (cf. Opp 2014, 89–96). Particularly when it comes to human behavior, scientific images of the futureoften do not refer to established social science theories, but instead make do with everyday theories. Social situations are more open and interpretation-oriented and therefore more susceptible to abrupt, unintended, and unforeseen shifts. Publicly negotiated images of the future also develop a momentum of their own, which can both promote and inhibit the occurrence of what is predicted (Merton 1948; see also the recent literature on imaginaries, e.g., Jasanoff and Kim 2015; Beckert and Bronk 2018). Finally, the ability to quickly and easily access the required data is limited; planning and conducting a survey study, for example, takes time.

Over the centuries, forecasters have used various strategies to lend authority and credibility to their knowledge claims despite these problems.[3] And the differences between the two knowledge collectives discussed in this book, futures studies and the sociology of problems, can be explained by reference to how exactly they positioned themselves vis-à-vis Thalesian and Beheimian allegations. From the very beginning, the majority of practitioners conceived of futures studies more as a scientific-intellectual movement, or an epistemic community, than a normal social scientific discipline. Since futures can be better or worse, and images of the future inform our decisions today, futures studies never seriously tried to make the case that it is value-neutral. Quite to the contrary, it was also quite open about the implications of this: to the proponents of futures studies, it simply made no sense to conceive of conducting such studies on the national level alone. While large parts of the social sciences were and still are nationally organized, futures studies from the very beginning was organized as an international endeavor. What is more, they deliberately sought the proximity of decision-makers, first in politics, but then, in order to increase their range of customers, also in the form of advising companies and other forms of business.

To large parts of the social sciences, this stance of futures studies was too close, and they themselves sometimes made Beheimian allegations to ridicule the results of futures studies as superficial and substance-less legitimation of the interests of paying clients. In return, their continued belief in the value of academic disciplines sometimes put them in the center of the Thalesian allegation to produce knowledge without any relevance or value for society.

Their different stances in how to best avoid Thalesian and Beheimian allegations, and their resulting social forms, have left traces on the social shapes of futures studies and the sociology of the future. While societal tensions have acted (and are acting and will act) as historical drivers of the social sciences, they have challenged (and partly destroyed) the internal coherence and cohesion of social science disciplines. The change in the form and organization of science in times of crisis often causes an unexpected surge of innovation in the sciences; however, it comes at the expense of the disciplinary organization of science. In times of crisis, such a transformation may be imperative—politically, socially, and academically

---

[3] More recently, these strategies have been bundled together and studied as "cultures of prediction" (Fine 2007; Daipha 2015; Heymann et al. 2017; Pietruska 2018). This research shows how actors culturally embed their predictions in order to socially stabilize the knowledge claims they contain and lend them credibility.

(Wallerstein et al. 1996). If, however, it becomes the major organizational principle in the sciences, this will entail a noticeable loss of knowledge and communication resources. Obviously, given its nature as a sub-discipline, this is a much bigger problem for the sociology of the future than for futures studies.

Trust in Experts, Trust in Numbers

To briefly recap what has been discussed at length in Chap. 2, social scientific interest in the future draws on a variety of sources, most of which originate in Europe. In the first decades of the twentieth century, thinkers such as H. G. Wells and Ossip K. Flechtheim repeatedly called for the establishment of foresight or futurology as an academic subject and emphasized its importance for society (Flechtheim 1971; see also Keßler 2007, 2011; Miles 2010). The best-known futurology theorists of the twentieth century—Robert Jungk (1952), Fritz Baade (1960), Denis Gabor (1963), Johan Galtung (Jungk and Galtung 1969), or Bertrand de Jouvenel (1967; 1968; see also Colquhoun 1996)—were Europeans. And yet, it were initiatives in the United States during the onset of the Cold War strengthened the empirical capacities of scientific foresight and developed methods that seemed appropriate for the tasks at hand. These initiatives, and the financial, intellectual, and organizational resources behind them, led to the consolidation of the previously scattered approaches and the establishment of futures studies as a scientific field (Andersson 2018). The timing is no coincidence: the fear of a global nuclear war turned the future into a vanishing point of uncertainty. As a way of coping with this uncertainty, "foreknowledge" gained in importance, not only in the field of military-political strategy planning but also in cultural terms. The meaning and content of ideas about the future are an expression of a social or cultural tension, and during the Cold War this took place in a global frame of reference (Seefried 2015; Andersson and Rindzevičiūtė 2015; Eberspächer 2019).

One reaction to nuclear uncertainty was the rise of a very specific social type or role, namely, that of the expert. As a quick glance at history shows, this is nothing new in terms of structure: in uncertain times, people look for authorities they can trust and then do so with an exuberant enthusiasm that can only appear misguided to those who come after them but also to some of their contemporaries. Nor can the fact that experts were consulted in this search be considered a novelty. What is historically new about this rise of the experts, however, is the fact that the trust in the experts' ability to find solutions was not only to be found in elite circles, but rather could rely on a broad social basis. Mass media and popular culture all hailed the expert. The heyday of the expert in the 1950s and 1960s was also a heyday of general enthusiasm for science, and the expert acted as a mediator, a translator, a link between the solution-producing machine of science and the society that demanded it (Collins 2014).

In this context, the quest for a middle way between Thales and Beheim sometimes found manifestation in using experts as sources for numeric estimates. The public trust in expertise thus joined forces with the public trust in numbers (Porter 1995). This applies to the Delphi survey as well as to the cross-impact matrix, simulations, and game theory-inspired experiments—in other words, to virtually all those methods that emerged from within futures studies (Tolon 2012; Dayé 2016). In Delphi surveys at RAND and elsewhere, experts from the natural sciences and technology were asked which innovations they expected to see in the next ten to twenty years. For the resulting list compiled from all the responses, they were asked to indicate in repeated questionnaires in which year they thought each of these innovations could be expected. As feedback, they received the median and quartiles of the estimates of all respondents from the preliminary round. This gave the experts the opportunity to reconsider their initial assessments (Linstone and Turoff 1975; Cuhls 1998; Häder 2009; Dayé 2018a).

Experts were thus more than mediators between science and society. Rather, they were elevated to a source of scientific knowledge. In a very concrete sense, their knowledge became part of the empiricism to be measured (cf. e.g., Helmer and Rescher 1959). The widespread hope in society that experts could show the way out of uncertainty was reflected at the level of social science methodology, where it determined thinking about possible forecasting techniques.

Social Demand and Its Consequences

In the early years of the Cold War, increased demand from decision-makers for social science expertise completely changed the rules of the game for a career in sociology. Suddenly, there was money outside the established structures of universities and local welfare organizations: jobs at think tanks, government agencies, or private (survey) companies (Igo 2007) promised not only high salaries but also contacts with those in power. In

The Sociological Imagination from 1959, C. Wright Mills described the new situation pointedly:

> For the first time in the history of their disciplines, social scientists have come into professional relations with private and public powers well above the level of the welfare agency and the county agent. Their positions change—from the academic to the bureaucratic; their publics change—from movements of reformers to circles of decisionmakers; and their problems change—from those of their own choice to those of their new clients. (Mills 2000, 95–6)

At the same time, the shape of social science knowledge changed. The demand for social science expertise at the beginning of the Cold War fed processes that had already been set in motion twenty years earlier: increasing quantification, an instrumental understanding of the role of theory, and a shoulder-shrugging nod to research results whose usefulness was not immediately apparent, but to which potential was ascribed. This also promoted the rise of experts, who were many things, but one thing they were not: mere academics. Experts were and are genuinely interstitial figures—they move between different social systems. And their knowledge is ultimately not framed by discipline, but by subject matter: they are not experts in sociology, but in poverty, for example.

The demand for sociological expertise created by the Cold War was not the actual cause of the tensions that characterized US sociology in the 1950s and 1960s—much more important were other social and cultural phenomena such as racism and anti-feminism, which were countered by the Civil Rights Act of 1964, and of course the controversies surrounding the proliferation of the capitalist form of production and which social system was ultimately fairer (Calhoun 2007). However, the demand for social science expertise on the part of decision-makers often served as a kind of convex lens in which resentment about the aforementioned grievances was bundled and ignited. Instead of addressing the problems of the population, the social sciences, and among them "fat-cat sociology" (Nicolaus 1991 [1968]), would chase after the big money of the state and economic elites. Instead of seeking access to the American population, they would—just as servilely as naively—work for the agendas of the military-political elites, for example, in the infamous Project Camelot (Horowitz 1967; Herman 1998; Solovey 2001; Navarro 2011). The social tensions of the 1950s and 1960s were thus not only incorporated into the social science discourse, which would come as no surprise, but also expanded to include fundamental and sometimes fierce controversies about the epistemological nature and social role of the social sciences, about the current and desirable form of social science knowledge production, and about the value of interdisciplinarity.

It was these ongoing controversies, and the reputational risks implied with being publicly attributed to one side in these controversies, that fostered the bipartite institutionalization of futures studies and the sociology of the future. As we have seen, although the bipartite institutionalization was at first expected to work as a bridge between different knowledge collectives, it eventually led to segregation into two attention spaces, with two different sets of intellectual lineages and few shared points of reference.

Detrimental Effects of Interdisciplinarity

The controversies mentioned above were fought out in various places, at universities (Isaac 2012), in university research groups (Fleck 2011; Cohen-Cole 2014), as well as in publications (Haney 2008)—just think of the book by C. Wright Mills (2000) cited above. But in some ways, these were sideshows. Unlike in many other controversies about the shape of the social sciences, such as the value judgment controversy (Albert 2011; Fleck 2020) or later the positivism controversy (Adorno et al. 1972; Ritsert 2011; Ploder 2020), this historical phase also involved social actors with considerable financial clout, in particular state and philanthropic research funding institutions (Parmar 2002, 2012; Hauptmann 2012; Solovey 2013, 2020; Jong 2020), think tanks (Rohde 2013; Dayé 2020; Ricci 1993, 2004; Medvetz 2012), but also supranational actors such as UNESCO (Wisselgren 2018, 2021; Fajardo 2021). These called for and promoted a methodological but also an organizational restructuring of the social sciences. In the 1960s, for example, the National Science Foundation, the most important state funding institution for basic research in the United States, only supported projects in the social sciences that were methodologically and theoretically in line with its ideas. With "behavioral sciences," the NSF even adopted a term created by the Ford Foundation for research that it considered worthy of funding (Fleck 2007; Pooley 2016; Solovey 2020).

The question of how social sciences should be organized was thus no longer only negotiated within the sciences, but became a social issue. At the same time, it was linked to the allocation of resources. The transformation process thus initiated was largely at the expense of the discipline as an organizational form. Other social forms, in particular the interdisciplinary working group, appeared far better suited to making contributions to understanding or solving the current problem situation. In contrast, the maintenance and further development of a disciplinary body of knowledge was of secondary importance. The emergence of futures studies as an international epistemic community that explicitly sought the proximity to decision-makers in polity and business can only be understood against this background.

In phases of social tension, the hopes placed in them lead social scientists to put methodological sophistication on the back burner in favor of quickly produced, action-guiding results. The result is a situation that could perhaps be pointedly described as a dialectic between diligence and sorrow and which is constituted by the difficult task of having to find a good place between the poles of quality assurance and speed of reaction. This can succeed, and together with the social significance of science, this can lead to a strong influx of people and resources for a certain period of time (Turner and Turner 1990). In fact, times of crisis have often also led to spurts of innovation in the sciences, which in all likelihood can be attributed to the creation of areas of interdisciplinary exchange, sometimes called *trading zones* (Galison 1997; Gorman 2002, 2010). The methods mentioned provide support for this assumption. A large part of the techniques still used today in futurology have their origins in the Cold War, and the same applies to the much larger part of the social sciences that are not prognostic in the narrower sense.

In the search for a good place in the field of tension between diligence and sorrow, however, a third task is pushed into the background. This is the linking of new findings and other innovations back to the disciplinary body of knowledge with the aim of integrating them theoretically and thus also further developing the original discipline. If the crisis arrangement becomes a model and the spaces of interdisciplinary exchange become permanent, then the link back to the respective disciplinary body of knowledge tends to fail, which can have destructive consequences for the discipline as an organizational form and knowledge container.

Social scientists will find themselves in new collaborations, will be confronted with new approaches in areas that they are not yet familiar with, and will receive considerable impetus from these interdisciplinary encounters. However, these developments could prove to be a further contribution to the centrifugal tendencies that exist within the discipline of sociology, for example, and which I would like to list as follows, following authors such as Andrew Abbott, James House, Jerry Jacobs, Stephen Turner, Frédéric Vandenberghe, and Stephan Fuchs:

- the fragmentation of social science disciplines into sub-disciplinary specialties;
- the rise and academic establishment of interdisciplinary fields of research such as science studies or gender studies; and
- the increasing adoption of activist aspects in academic practice (cf. Abbott 2001; Jacobs 2014; Turner 2014; House 2019; Vandenberghe and Fuchs 2019).

These centrifugal tendencies present sociology with challenges that it may not be able to meet if it sticks to its organization as a discipline. The problem is not that sociology has a multi-paradigmatic character and does not pursue a largely shared theoretical program. This is neither a specific feature of sociology nor has it proved to be an obstacle in recent decades. The problem lies in the fact that there is hardly any interest in and certainly hardly any gratification for the feedback of one's own results to the disciplinary reservoir of knowledge. In terms of the social organization of its attention space, futures studies are better suited to adapt to changes on the demand side—but on the other hand, they suffer from a lack of stabilization that result from a consistence of being organized as a discipline.

Perhaps the academic discipline as a form of organization in the social sciences is outdated. In any case, it does not seem to correspond to the current interests of many actors, nor to the demands on science that society usually makes in times of crisis. Perhaps other forms of organization will not only dominate knowledge production in the future but also take over academic reproduction and jurisdiction (Abbott 1988). That may be the way of things, and who wants to stand in its way? However, it is obvious that a lot will be lost in the process. If the link to existing knowledge is no longer systematically implemented, demanded, and sanctioned, it will disappear from the "working memory" of the social sciences (Swedberg 2012, 2013).

Not surprisingly, the lack of a working memory in futures studies is often lamented by its practitioners. Comparing the results from Chaps. 5 and 6, we can see that in contrast to the sociology of the future, the epistemic tribes of futures studies also address an audience that is primarily more interested in taking good decisions than in increasing the available body of knowledge: epistemic tribe #4 is specifically interested in using scenarios in strategic planning, and its intended audiences presumably extend beyond scientists to include policy-makers, business managers, and members of the civil and military services. This tribe, however, has a conflict-laden relationship to epistemic tribe #5 in futures studies, a tribe that was interpreted as trying to push futures studies more into the shape of a scientific discipline and thus closer to other social sciences.

Conclusion: Two Fields of Social Scientific Futures Thinking

The empirical studies presented in this book show that in terms of intellectual reference points, there is factually no overlap between futures studies and the sociology of the future. The epistemic tribes dominating each of these knowledge collectives claim different lineages, and by and large also different territories.

There are several ways to evaluate these findings. On the one hand, observers might say that in terms of intellectual development, this situation is bad, as a lack of common sources and the concomitant lack of a shared repertoire hampers a fruitful dialogue between these two fields. On the other hand, however, one could also argue that the dominance of sociological reference points in the sociology of the future indicates a valuable stubbornness of sociologists to maintain their disciplinary belonging. In a situation characterized by a continued crisis mode, the future of the social science disciplines depends on whether those currently conducting social science research are willing to undergo the effort of reconnecting with the respective disciplinary bodies of knowledge—and whether they are given the necessary resources to do so.

Yet, based on this, a third interpretation might be most productive, as it directs the view toward the future. Perhaps the way forward is not to integrate these two fields but to acknowledge that they somehow present two answers to the societal pressures that impact science and to use yet-to-be established places of dialogue—*trading zones*—not to unify them but to better exploit the capacities that arise from this difference. An ideal would be some form of tacit contractual arrangement between the two, where a diligent division of labor increases the productivity of both and the quality of their products. If there existed more suitable trading zones, both sides would profit by an increased awareness of theories and topics that are debated by the other, as this awareness would allow them to concentrate on their tasks more efficiently and jointly provide a more balanced form of futures thinking that combines answering societal demands with maintaining disciplinary stability.

References

Abbott, Andrew. 1988. *The System of Professions: An Essay on the Division of Expert Labor*. Chicago: University of Chicago Press.
Abbott, Andrew. 2001. *Chaos of Disciplines*. Chicago and London: The University of Chicago Press.
Adorno, Theodor W., Ralf Dahrendorf, Harald Pilot, Hans Albert, Jürgen Habermas, and Karl R. Popper. 1972. *Der Positivismusstreit in der deutschen Soziologie*. Neuwied, Berlin: Luchterhand.
Albert, Gert. 2011. Der Werturteilsstreit. In *Soziologische Kontroversen*, ed. Georg Kneer and Stephan Moebius, 14–45. Frankfurt am Main: Suhrkamp.
Andersson, Jenny. 2018. *The Future of the World: Futurology, Futurists, and the Struggle for the Post Cold War Imagination*. Oxford, New York: Oxford University Press.
Andersson, Jenny, and Eglė Rindzevičiūtė, ed. 2015. *The Struggle for the Long-Term in Transnational Science and Politics: Forging the Future*. Routledge Approaches to History 11. New York, London: Routledge.
Baade, Fritz. 1960. *Der Wettlauf zum Jahre 2000. Paradies oder Selbstvernichtung*. Oldenburg, Hamburg: Gerhard Stalling.
Beckert, Jens, and Richard Bronk, eds. 2018. *Uncertain Futures: Imaginaries, Narratives, and Calculation in the Economy*. Oxford: Oxford University Press.
Bell, Wendell. 2003. *Foundations of Futures Studies. Volume 1: History, Purposes, and Knowledge*. 2nd ed. Human Science for a New Era 1. New Brunswick, NJ: Transaction Publishers.
Blumenberg, Hans. 1987. *Das Lachen der Thrakerin. Eine Urgeschichte der Theorie*. Frankfurt am Main: Suhrkamp.
Calhoun, Craig, ed. 2007. *Sociology in America: A History*. Chicago, London: The University of Chicago Press.
Cohen-Cole, Jamie. 2014. *The Open Mind: Cold War Politics and the Sciences of Human Nature*. Chicago, London: The University of Chicago Press.
Collins, Harry. 2014. *Are We All Scientific Experts Now?* Cambridge (UK), Malden (MA): Polity Press.
Colquhoun, Robert. 1996. The Art of Social Conjecture: Remembering Bertrand de Jouvenel. *History of the Human Sciences* 9:27–42.
Cuhls, Kerstin. 1998. *Technikvorausschau in Japan. Ein Rückblick auf 30 Jahre Delphi-Expertenbefragungen*. Berlin, Heidelberg: Springer.

Daipha, Phaedra. 2015. *Masters of Uncertainty: Weather Forecasters and the Quest for Ground Truth*. Chicago, London: University of Chicago Press.

Dayé, Christian. 2016. 'A Fiction of Long Standing': Techniques of Prospection and the Role of Positivism in US Cold War Social Science, 1950–65. *History of the Human Sciences* 29:35–58. https://doi.org/10.1177/0952695116664838.

Dayé, Christian. 2018a. How to Train Your Oracle: The Delphi Method and Its Turbulent Youth in Operations Research and the Policy Sciences. *Social Studies of Science* 48:846–868. https://doi.org/10.1177/0306312718798497.

Dayé, Christian. 2020. *Experts, Social Scientists, and Techniques of Prognosis in Cold War America*. Cham, CH: Palgrave Macmillan.

Eberspächer, Achim. 2019. *Das Projekt Futurologie: Über Zukunft und Fortschritt in der Bundesrepublik 1952–1982*. Leiden, Boston: Brill Schöningh.

Fajardo, Margarita. 2021. Latin America's Dependency Theory: A Counter-Cold War Social Science? In *Cold War Social Science: Transnational Entanglements*, ed. Mark Solovey and Christian Dayé, 191–222. Cham: Palgrave Macmillan.

Fine, Gary Alan. 2007. *Authors of the storm: Meteorologists and the Culture of Prediction*. Chicago: The University of Chicago Press.

Flechtheim, Ossip K. 1971. *Futurologie. Der Kampf um die Zukunft*. 2. Auflage. Köln: Verlag Wissenschaft und Politik.

Fleck, Christian. 2007. *Transatlantische Bereicherungen. Zur Erfindung der empirischen Sozialforschung*. Frankfurt am Main: Suhrkamp.

Fleck, Christian. 2011. *A Transatlantic History of the Social Sciences: Robber Barons, the Third Reich and the Invention of Empirical Social Research*. Translated by Hella Beister. London; New York: Bloomsbury Academic.

Fleck, Christian. 2020. Werturteilsfreiheit. In *Meilensteine der Soziologie*, ed. Christian Fleck and Christian Dayé, 183–192. Frankfurt am Main, New York: Campus.

Gabor, Dennis. 1963. *Inventing the Future*. London: Secker and Warburg.

Galison, Peter. 1997. *Image and Logic. A Material Culture of Microphysics*. Chicago and London: Chicago University Press.

Gorman, Michael E. 2002. Levels of Expertise and Trading Zones: A Framework for Multidisciplinary Collaboration. *Social Studies of Science* 32:933–938.

Gorman, Michael E., ed. 2010. *Trading Zones and Interactional Expertise: Creating New Kinds of Collaboration*. Boston (MA): MIT Press.

Häder, Michael. 2009. *Delphi-Befragungen. Ein Arbeitsbuch*. Wiesbaden: VS Verlag für Sozialwissenschaften.

Haney, David Paul. 2008. *The Americanization of Social Science: Intellectuals and Public Responsibility in the Postwar United States*. Philadelphia: Temple University Press.

Hauptmann, Emily. 2012. The Ford Foundation and the Rise of Behavioralism in Political Science. *Journal of the History of the Behavioral Sciences* 48:154–173. https://doi.org/10.1002/jhbs.21515.

Helmer, Olaf, and Nicholas Rescher. 1959. On the Epistemology of the Inexact Sciences. *Management Science* 6:25–52.

Herman, Ellen. 1998. Project Camelot and the Career of Cold War Psychology. In *University and Empire: Money and Politics in the Social Sciences During the Cold War*, ed. Christopher Simpson, 39–56. New York: The New Press.

Heymann, Matthias, Gabriele Gramelsberger, and Martin Mahony, eds. 2017. *Cultures of Prediction in Atmospheric and Climate Science: Epistemic and Cultural Shifts in Computer-based Modelling and Simulation*. Milton Park, New York: Routledge.

Horowitz, Irving Louis, ed. 1967. *The Rise and Fall of Project Camelot: Studies in the Relationship between Social Science and Practical Politics.* Cambridge, MA: M.I.T. Press.

House, James S. 2019. The Culminating Crisis of American Sociology and Its Role in Social Science and Public Policy: An Autobiographical, Multimethod, Reflexive Perspective. *Annual Review of Sociology* 45:1–26. https://doi.org/10.1146/annurev-soc-073117-041052.

Igo, Sarah E. 2007. *The Averaged American. Surveys, Citizens, and the Making of a Mass Public*. Cambridge (MA), London: Harvard University Press.

Isaac, Joel. 2012. *Working Knowledge: Making the Human Sciences from Parsons to Kuhn*. Cambridge, MA: Harvard University Press.

Jacobs, Jerry A. 2014. *In Defense of Disciplines: Interdisciplinarity and Specialization in the Research University*. Chicago, London: The University of Chicago Press.

Jasanoff, Sheila, and Sang-Hyun Kim. 2015. *Dreamscapes of Modernity: Sociotechnical Imaginaries and the Fabrication of Power*. Chicago, London: The University of Chicago Press.

Jong, Willem Pieter Theodoor (Wim) De. 2020. Cold War Social Science in Action. The Ford Foundation and Liberal Adult Education in the United States (1945-60). *Cold War History* 20:399–418. https://doi.org/10.1080/14682745.2019.1673737.

Jouvenel, Bertrand de. 1967. *The Art of Conjecture*. New York: Basic Books.

Jouvenel, Bertrand de. 1968. Notes on Social Forecasting. In *Forecasting and the Social Sciences*, ed. Michael Young, 118–134. London: Heinemann.

Jungk, Robert. 1952. Die Zukunft hat schon begonnen. In *Amerikas Allmacht und Ohnmacht*. Bern, Stuttgart: Alfred Scherz.

Jungk, Robert, and Johan Galtung, eds. 1969. *Mankind 2000*. Oslo: Universitetsforlaget.

Keßler, Mario. 2007. *Ossip K. Flechtheim: politischer Wissenschaftler und Zukunftsdenker (1909–1998)*. Köln: Böhlau.
Keßler, Mario. 2011. Zur Futurologie von Ossip K. Flechtheim. In *Macht und Geist im Kalten Krieg*, ed. Bernd Greiner, Tim B. Müller, and Claudia Weber, 239–257. Hamburg: Hamburger Edition.
Linstone, Harold A., and Murray Turoff. 1975. *The Delphi Method. Techniques and Applications*. London, Reading (MA): Addison-Wesley.
Medvetz, Thomas. 2012. *Think Tanks in America*. Chicago, London: The University of Chicago Press.
Merton, Robert K. 1948. The Self-Fulfilling Prophecy. *The Antioch Review* 8:193–210.
Merton, Robert K. 1996. The Ethos of Science. In *On Social Structure and Science*, ed. and with an Introduction by Piotr Sztompka, 267–276. Chicago: The University of Chicago Press.
Miles, Ian. 2010. The Development of Technology Foresight: A Review. *Technological Forecasting and Social Change* 77:1448–1456. https://doi.org/10.1016/j.techfore.2010.07.016.
Mills, C. Wright. 2000. *The Sociological Imagination*. Oxford, New York: Oxford University Press.
Navarro, Juan José. 2011. Cold War in Latin America: The Camelot Project (1964-1965) and the Political and Academic Reactions of the Chilean Left. *Comparative Sociology* 10:807–825.
Nicolaus, Martin. 1991. Fat-Cat Sociology. In *Radical Sociologists and the Movement: Experiences, Lessons, and Legacies*, ed. Martin Oppenheimer, Martin J. Murray, and Rhonda F. Levine, 251–254. Philadelphia: Temple University Press.
Opp. 2014. *Methodologie*. VS Verlag für Sozialwissenschaften.
Panofsky, Aaron L. 2010. A Critical Reconsideration of the Ethos and Autonomy of Science. In *Robert K. Merton: Sociology of Science and Sociology as Science*, ed. Craig J. Calhoun, 140–163. New York: Columbia University Press.
Parmar, Inderjeet. 2002. American Foundations and the Development of International Knowledge Networks. *Global Networks* 2:13–30.
Parmar, Inderjeet. 2012. *Foundations of the American Century: The Ford, Carnegie, and Rockefeller Foundations in the Rise of American Power*. Reprint: Columbia University Press.
Pietruska, Jamie L. 2018. *Looking Forward: Prediction & Uncertainty in Modern America*. Chicago: University of Chicago Press.
Ploder, Andrea. 2020. Positivismus und Anti-Positivismus. In *Meilensteine der Soziologie*, ed. Christian Fleck and Christian Dayé, 438–446. Frankfurt am Main, New York: Campus.

Pooley, Jefferson D. 2016. A "Not Particularly Felicitous" Phrase: A History of the "Behavioral Sciences" Label. *Serendipities - Journal for the Sociology and History of the Social Sciences* 1:38–81.

Porter, Theodore M. 1995. *Trust in Numbers. The Pursuit of Objectivity in Science and Public Life.* Princeton (NJ): Princeton University Press.

Ricci, David M. 1993. *The Transformation of American Politics. The New Washington and the Rise of Think Tanks.* New Haven, London: Yale University Press.

Rich, Andrew. 2004. *Think Tanks, Public Policy, and the Politics of Expertise.* Cambridge, New York, Melbourne: Cambridge University Press.

Ritsert, Jürgen. 2011. Der Positivismusstreit. In *Soziologische Kontroversen*, ed. Georg Kneer and Stephan Moebius, 102–130. Frankfurt am Main: Suhrkamp.

Rohde, Joy. 2013. *Armed with Expertise: The Militarization of American Social Research During the Cold War.* Ithaca, London: Cornell University Press.

Seefried, Elke. 2015. *Zukünfte. Aufstieg und Krise der Zukunftsforschung 1945–1980.* Berlin: Walter de Gruyter.

Solovey, Mark. 2001. Project Camelot and the 1960s Epistemological Revolution: Rethinking the Politics-patronage-social Science Nexus. *Social Studies of Science* 31:171–206.

Solovey, Mark. 2013. *Shaky Foundations: The Politics-Patronage-Social Science Nexus in Cold War America.* New Brunswick, N.J: Rutgers University Press.

Solovey, Mark. 2020. *Social Science for What?: Battles over Public Funding for the "Other Sciences" at the National Science Foundation.* Cambridge, Massachusetts: The MIT Press.

Swedberg, Richard. 2012. History of Sociology as the Working Memory of Sociology. *Timelines: Newsletter of the ASA History of Sociology Section* 20: 1:11–12.

Swedberg, Richard. 2013. History of Sociology as the Working Memory of Sociology (Part 2). *Timelines: Newsletter of the ASA History of Sociology Section* 21:1–2, 20–21.

Tolon, Kaya. 2012. Future Studies: A New Social Science Rooted in Cold War Strategic Thinking. In *Cold War Social Science: Knowledge Production, Liberal Democracy, and Human Nature*, ed. Mark Solovey and Hamilton Cravens, 45–62. New York: Palgrave Macmillan.

Turner, Stephen. 2014. *American Sociology: From Pre-disciplinary to Post-normal.* Sociology transformed. Basingstoke: Palgrave Macmillan.

Turner, Stephen Park, and Jonathan H. Turner. 1990. *The Impossible Science: An Institutional Analysis of American Sociology.* Newbury Park, London, New Delhi: Sage.

Vandenberghe, Frédéric, and Stephan Fuchs. 2019. On the Coming End of Sociology. *Canadian Review of Sociology/Revue canadienne de sociologie* 56:138–143. https://doi.org/10.1111/cars.12238.

Wallerstein, Immanuel, Calestous Juma, Evelyn Fox Keller, Jürgen Kocka, Dominique Lecourt, V. Y. Mudkimbe, Kinhide Miushakoji, Ilya Prigogine, Peter J. Taylor, and Michel-Rolph Trouillot. 1996. *Open the Social Sciences: Report of the Gulbenkian Commission on the Restructuring of the Social Sciences*. Mestizo Spaces - Espaces Métisses. Stanford (CA): Stanford University Press.

Wisselgren, Per. 2018. From Utopian One-worldism to Geopolitical Intergovernmentalism: UNESCO'S Department of Social Sciences as an International Boundary Organization, 1946–1955. *Serendipities* 2:148–182.

Author Index[1]

A
Adam, Barbara, 88, 90, 91

B
Bacon, Lord Francis, 7, 101
Becher, Tony, 36, 38, 41, 42, 59
Beck, Ulrich, 86, 90
Beckert, Jens, 60, 60n1, 88, 90
Beheim, Michael, 100, 104
Bell, Daniel, 26
Bell, Wendell, 20, 21, 64, 65, 70, 71, 76, 91, 100
Bellamy, Edward, 7
Benson, Robert Hugh, 8
Berger, Gaston, 25, 26
Berger, Peter L., 89
Berlant, Lauren, 91
Bestuzhev-Lada, Igor, 27, 28
Bloomfield, Lincoln P., 25
Bourdieu, Pierre, 3, 52

C
Campanella, Tommaso, 6
Collins, Randall, 47, 58
Comte, Auguste, 101
Crane, Diana, 37, 45, 46

D
Dalkey, Norman C., 22, 23
Dator, Jim, 28, 73
Durkheim, Émile, 89

F
Farrell, Michael P., 37, 49, 50
Flechtheim, Ossip K., 9, 15–21, 103
Fleck, Ludwik, 36, 38, 39, 43, 44, 106
Foucault, Michel, 37, 90, 91
Franck, Georg, 58
Frickel, Scott, 37, 51, 52

[1] Note: Page numbers followed by 'n' refer to notes.

G

Gabor, Dennis, 15–21, 24, 103
Galtung, Johan, 4, 27, 103
Garfinkel, Harold, 89
Giddens, Anthony, 76, 90, 91
Gidley, Jennifer, 2
Goffman, Erving, 89
Goldhamer, Herbert, 22, 24
Gordon, Theodore J., 24, 69
Gross, Neil, 37, 51, 52
Grove, Chris, 88, 91

H

Hagstrom, Warren O., 37, 44, 45
Helmer, Olaf, 14, 17n3, 22–24, 27, 69, 104
Humboldt, Alexander von, 9
Huxley, Aldous, 8

I

Inayatullah, Soheil, 4, 73

J

Jouvenel, Bertrand de, 20, 24, 26–28, 74, 103
Jouvenel, François de, 26
Jouvenel, Hugues de, 25, 26
Jungk, Robert, 15–21, 25, 27, 40, 76, 103

K

Kahn, Herman, 22, 23, 26, 27, 69, 70, 76
Kecskemeti, Paul, 22, 24
Knorr Cetina, Karin, 36, 38, 42, 42n3
Kuhn, Thomas S., 38, 44, 45, 47, 48

Kurzweil, Ray, 74

L

Luckmann, Thomas, 89

M

Marx, Karl, 7, 89
Merton, Robert K., 15, 44, 45, 100, 101
Miller, Riel, 70, 73
Mills, C. Wright, 89, 105, 106
Mische, Ann, 86, 90
More, Sir Thomas, 6
Morrison, Jim, 2

O

Ozbeckhan, Hasan, 26

P

Parsons, Talcott, 89
Polak, Fred L., 74
Polanyi, Karl, 90
Poli, Roberto, 74

R

Rosten, Leo, 22, 23

S

Sardar, Ziauddin, 10, 27, 70, 71, 73
Schwartz, Peter, 65, 70
Seefried, Elke, 39, 40, 40n2, 71, 103
Shelly, Mary, 8
Speier, Hans, 22, 24
Suckert, Lisa, 60, 60n1

T
Thales of Miletus, 99
Tiryakian, Edward, 37, 47–49
Toffler, Alvin, 74
Trowler, Paul, 36, 41, 42, 52, 59

V
van der Heijden, Kees, 70

van Eck, Nees Jan, 62
Verne, Jules, 8, 18

W
Waltman, Ludo, 62
Weber, Max, 3, 16, 88, 89
Wells, H. G., 8, 69, 103
Wiener, Anthony, 23, 70, 76

Subject Index[1]

A

Academic tribes and territories (Becher), 36, 38, 40–42
Attention space, 57–65, 70, 71, 74, 76, 79, 84, 86, 90, 91, 94, 97, 106, 108
Augurs, 5

C

Co-citation analysis, 58, 61–63, 65, 70, 71, 86
Collaborative circle, 37, 49–50
Co-occurrence analysis, 58, 61, 62, 65, 91, 94

D

Delphi
  the oracle, 5
  research method, 25

E

Epistemic community (Haas), 37, 51–53, 102, 107
Epistemic culture (Knorr Cetina), 36, 38, 42–43, 42–43n3
Epistemic tribes and territories, 2, 10, 42, 57–65, 69–81, 83–97, 108, 109
Experts, 14, 23–25, 51, 103–105

F

Ford Foundation, 26, 106
Forecast, 8, 14
Foresight, 3–5, 10, 73, 77, 79, 89, 90, 101, 103
Future
  the idea of the, 3–10, 15, 18, 40, 70, 103
  images of the, 2, 8, 9, 14, 20, 40, 70, 71, 74, 79, 93, 97, 102
  workshop, 25, 40

---

[1] Note: Page numbers followed by 'n' refer to notes.

Futuribles, 25–28
Futurology, 10, 14, 16–20, 64, 69, 70, 76, 103, 107

H
Hawaii Research Center for Futures Studies, 28
Hudson Institute, 27

I
Institute for the Future (IFTF), 27, 28
Institutionalization, bipartite, 2, 10, 28–29, 35–36, 106
Invisible college, 37, 43, 45–46

M
Macrohistory, 4
Mont Pélerin Society, 26

P
Political gaming, 22, 24, 25
Pythia, 5

R
RAND Corporation, 19, 22, 26

S
Scenario analysis, 22, 23, 25
Scenarios, 22–25, 71, 74, 79, 109
Scientific community, 37, 38, 43, 45, 46
Scientific/intellectual movements (Frickel & Gross), 37, 51–52
Scientific school, 37–49, 76
Systems analysis, 22

T
Technological progress, 2, 8, 9
Thought collective and thought style, 36, 38–40, 42, 44
Time, 2, 3n2, 5–7, 15, 22, 23, 25, 26, 28, 37, 40, 45, 46, 48, 52, 58, 59, 63, 69–71, 79, 93–95, 97, 101–103, 105–108
Trading zones, 107, 109

U
UNESCO, 27, 28, 106
Utopia, 6–9, 16, 101

W
World Future Society, 27, 28
World Futures Studies Federation (WFSF), 25–28

Printed in the United States
by Baker & Taylor Publisher Services